PRAISE FOR *TALKING TO SPIRITS*

"Not many books have spoken directly and clearly about the art of spirit communication in a digestible and informative way until now. *Talking to Spirits* ticks all the boxes for me. With each chapter, the very knowledgeable Sterling Moon gently guides you. She is not only a formidable tarot reader, but also a very attuned medium and educator of the magical arts. I look forward to sharing this book as a resource with my clients and others seeking to expand their own psyches." —**Marcella Kroll, creator of *The Sacred Symbols Oracle, The Nature Nurture Oracle, The Dreamers Tarot*, and *The Roast Iconic Oracle***

"A comprehensive manual on mediumship, *Talking to Spirits* is packed with a wealth of information for conversing with the dead. Even the smallest details are covered, starting with basic tenets of spirit communication before advancing into the murky world beyond the veil … Her personal experiences as a psychic medium have made her highly knowledgeable and her research is impeccable. Plus, it's written in such a genial, conversational tone, the reader will feel like Ms. Moon is their own personal tour guide to the other side." —**Pleasant Gehman, author of *Rock 'n' Roll Witch***

"While mediumship might seem intimidating for the uninitiated, *Talking to Spirits* teaches you this valuable spiritual skill in a totally approachable way. In her book, author Sterling Moon makes it easy to get to know the spirits and identify the ways they reach out to those of us in the physical realm … If you feel drawn to working in the spirit realm, you will come back to this book again and again for tips, tricks, and deep wisdom." —**Madame Pamita, author of *Baba Yaga's Book of Witchcraft, The Book of Candle Magic*, and *Madame Pamita's Magical Tarot***

TALKING
TO
SPIRITS

ABOUT THE AUTHOR

Sterling Moon has communicated with spirits since childhood and began officially practicing mediumship in 2016. She has been reading tarot since 1995 and teaching divination skills since 2013. She works with clients virtually and in-person at her private office in the metaphysical shop, Ritualcravt. She teaches through her school, Sterling Moon Divination Academy, and is a longtime instructor at Ritualcravt School. She also apprenticed under Johannes Björn Gårdbäck, an internationally respected teacher and spiritual worker in the Swedish folk magic tradition of trolldom. She lives in Colorado. Learn more about Sterling at sterlingmoontarot.com.

TO WRITE TO THE AUTHOR

If you wish to contact the author or would like more information about this book, please write to the author in care of Llewellyn Worldwide Ltd. and we will forward your request. Both the author and the publisher appreciate hearing from you and learning of your enjoyment of this book and how it has helped you. Llewellyn Worldwide Ltd. cannot guarantee that every letter written to the author can be answered, but all will be forwarded. Please write to:

Sterling Moon
℅ Llewellyn Worldwide
2143 Wooddale Drive
Woodbury, MN 55125-2989

Please enclose a self-addressed stamped envelope for reply,
or $1.00 to cover costs. If outside the U.S.A., enclose
an international postal reply coupon.

Many of Llewellyn's authors have websites with additional information and resources. For more information, please visit our website at http://www.llewellyn.com.

STERLING MOON

TALKING
TO
SPIRITS

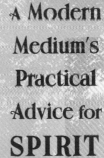

A Modern
Medium's
Practical
Advice for
SPIRIT
COMMUNICATION

LLEWELLYN PUBLICATIONS
Woodbury, Minnesota

FIRST EDITION
Second Printing, 2023

Book design by Christine Ha
Cover design by Shannon McKuhen

Llewellyn Publications is a registered trademark of Llewellyn Worldwide Ltd.

Library of Congress Cataloging-in-Publication Data
Names: Moon, Sterling, author.
Title: Talking to spirits : a modern medium's practical advice for spirit
    communication / Sterling Moon.
Description: First edition. | Woodbury, MN : Llewellyn Publications, a
    Division of Llewellyn Worldwide Ltd, 2022. | Includes bibliographical
    references.
Identifiers: LCCN 2022046747 (print) | LCCN 2022046748 (ebook) | ISBN
    9780738773476 | ISBN 9780738773551 (ebook)
Subjects: LCSH: Spiritualism.
Classification: LCC BF1261.2 M66 2023 (print) | LCC BF1261.2 (ebook) |
    DDC 133.9—dc23/eng/20221212
LC record available at https://lccn.loc.gov/2022046747
LC ebook record available at https://lccn.loc.gov/2022046748

Llewellyn Publications
A Division of Llewellyn Worldwide Ltd.
2143 Wooddale Drive
Woodbury, MN 55125-2989
www.llewellyn.com

Printed in the United States of America

CONTENTS

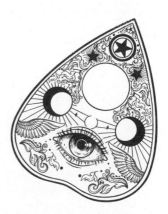

MEDITATION LIST

ACKNOWLEDGMENTS

This book is dedicated to "Mr. Moon" and "Lil Moon," also known as Scott "LB" Bergman and Townes. LB, thank you for believing that I can pull off my wild ideas and for loving me. Townes, thank you for being interested in what I was writing and reminding me when it was time to take a break. Writing while the two of you played *Zelda: Breath of the Wild* will remain a cherished memory. I love you both so very much.

This book is also dedicated to the memory of Dee Bergman, Dolly Harris, and Jayden Nash Alvarado. Remembering you brings me home to why this work matters.

Thank you to my mom, Kimberly Goodspeed Harris. You always let me be myself, even when I am a pain. Thank you for letting me develop my spiritual beliefs in my own way. I love you and am proud to be your daughter.

Thank you to my stepdad, Donovan Rudisuhle. You've been a gift to our family and I am not sure we would have embraced cryptozoology without you!

Thank you to my family on the other side, particularly my grandparents, Jane Marie Miller Goodspeed and Henry S. Goodspeed, and my father, Dale Allen Harris.

Thank you to Llewellyn for bringing me on as a first-time author. I am very appreciative of all the team members I have had the pleasure of working with, but especially Amy Glaser. Your encouragement, patience, and support made all the difference. Thank you so very much.

Acknowledgments

Thank you to Missy Rhysing. Hiring me as a House Reader back in 2016 changed the course of my life. Thank you for allowing me to be part of what you have created through Ritualcravt.

Thank you to Loretta Ledesma, one of the coolest women I know. You have taught me more than you likely realize, and I am so grateful for your friendship.

Thank you to Johannes Björn Gårdbäck. Studying with you was life changing. Thanks for being such a thoughtful and kind teacher … and for pushing me out into the world when you did.

Thank you to Danielle Battagione for being one of my early teachers and for reminding me that these gifts need to be treated with reverence.

Thank you to my besties outside of the magical community. Jessi Skarda and Shannon Leighton, I love you and our group chat keeps me grounded. Beth Malmskog, thank you for your unwavering support and friendship. Miriam Burke, thank you for setting an example of how an unusual life can also be a wonderful and fulfilling life. Lisa Luokkala, thanks for always providing a fresh perspective and no-nonsense advice. Kat Havlova Lewis, thank you for being so good to our family. I love you and James so very much.

Thank you to Heather Link-Bergman for being my favorite Virgo. Your keen eye and aesthetic has been making my writing look good since 2017.

Thank you to Dr. Lisa Martinez and Dr. Samuel Nez for your feedback on parts of this book and for your friendship over the years. You do so much for every community you are part of. Thank you for all of it.

Thank you to Molly McClellan for the herbz and your friend checks. They always came right when I needed them while I was writing this book.

Thank you to all the Ritualcravt witches who've come and gone over the years, with extra gratitude to Molly Brennan, Zach Horton, and Jess Ellis.

Thank you to Madame Pamita for your kind advice and support throughout this journey.

Thank you to Marcella Kroll and Pleasant Gehman for being among the first to read this book. I appreciate your kind words and friendship.

Thank you to Naomi Brodner. You threw me a lifeline when I most needed it. I will be forever grateful for your kindness and belief in me.

Thank you to Leah Parker for your wise advice when this book was just a general concept in my head. I am forever wishing you the best life has to offer.

Thank you to Mandee McLane and Ami McCarthy. Life has taken us in different directions, but you are still "ride or die" in my heart.

Last, but not least, thank you to my clients and students. I am forever grateful for the honor to sit with you.

INTRODUCTION

We all walk in a haunted world. It makes no difference if we believe in it or are attuned to it. Those who get a glimpse of what lies beyond the proverbial veil understand that there is far more to the world than what meets the eye. While skepticism is healthy and has its place, once you go down the path of learning to connect with the spirit world, you will encounter things that defy explanation. This book is here to support you in seeking out these strange and wonderful experiences.

If you have found yourself with this book in your hands, I suspect you are someone who

+ likes a good ghost story or magical tale,
+ knows or suspects they are sensitive to spirits of the dead or other spiritual beings, and/or
+ is interested in developing their intuition and ability to perceive and interact with spirits and the unseen world.

Many of you likely have your own history of spirit encounters. Some of you may wish to have these experiences and hope this book will bring you closer to that which often goes unseen. Maybe you are just curious about ghosts and hauntings and thought this book sounded like a fun, hair-raising read. My friends, this book is for all of you. We will cover everything you need to know to start developing your own personal practice of connecting with spirits. We will break down the most common types of spirits and how to identify them, how to train your mind and your intuition so you can better decipher messages from spirits, and the nitty-gritty of how to talk to

1

spirits and stay safe while doing so. I'll also tell a lot of good stories along the way.

Let's start by settling on what the heck mediumship even is. The simplest definition of mediumship is the practice of communicating with that which lies between—i.e., the spirit world. The person facilitating the communication is the medium. Mediums use a variety of communication methods. We will talk about many of them throughout this book, but the sky is the limit. You may even stumble upon a brand-new means of communication.

The way I practice and teach mediumship is guided by four primary influences:

- *Classic mediumship techniques.* Most mediums have similarities in how we work. We all have some sort of grounding practice. Most mediums cast a circle of sorts before we call in spirits, which provides protection from less-than-helpful entities and must be released when we are done. We all have ways we cleanse and release from the experience. Most of us use tools such as pendulums, tarot cards, scrying mirrors, candles, dowsing rods, and more. Some of us use techniques developed by practitioners of Spiritualism, which approaches communication with spirits as a religious practice, or we use techniques from classic books such as Raymond Buckland's *Book of Spirit Communications*.

- *Folk magic.* Folk magic encompasses the magical practices of everyday life. It helps us make the mundane magical. It is the opposite of ritualistic, ceremonial magic. Every culture in the world has some kind of magical practice that is unique to them and their region, yet there are incredible similarities. Folk magic practices help us become a conduit for divine power that can then be used in tandem with plants, the elements, planets, seasons, and more. Folk magic also involves partnership with those in the spiritual realm, whether they are spirits of the dead, earth spirits, deities, and more. My practice is heavily influenced by the Scandinavian folk magic tradition of trolldom, the folk practices of my Northern and Eastern European ancestors, and the teaching I have received in conjure and hoodoo, which are magical practices rooted in the Southern United States and were created by enslaved people of African descent. Not all mediums consider themselves magical practitioners, and not all magical practitioners call themselves mediums. I embrace both and would love to help more people do the same. I will reference magic frequently throughout this book. If that's not your bag, it's okay. I have parsed out the lessons that apply to spirit communication but cannot fully unbraid how my experience as a magical practitioner guides my work as a medium.

+ *Paranormal investigation.* I greatly appreciate the techniques and tools that have been developed by paranormal investigators. The field's focus on history, experimentation, and approaching spirit activity with a healthy dose of rational, left-brain skepticism provides a useful counterbalance to traditional mediumship techniques. I find tools such as spirit boxes, EVP (electronic voice phenomena) recordings, and EMF (electromagnetic field) meters particularly helpful when my abilities get tired or I encounter situations that are too confusing for me to parse out in my mind. This book will provide options for incorporating paranormal investigation tools and techniques into your own mediumship practices.

+ *Working with natural talents.* Anyone can learn to talk to spirits. While some of us come into the world with these skills dialed up, we all possess psychic senses that can be enhanced and strengthened. There is no one-size-fits-all method for how to do this. While we all want answers that can be neatly packaged, consumed, digested, and integrated, that is currently not possible when it comes to the spirit realm. None of us can 100 percent understand how this stuff works in a global sense, but we can get very attuned to how spirit communication works for us as individuals. We each have a secret sauce that will allow us to communicate with the other side. As we develop discernment and learn from our own experiences, we can figure out what allows our heightened senses to work at full capacity.

WHAT TO EXPECT FROM THIS BOOK

Everyone's mediumship practice will have nuances that are unique to them. This book will help you identify the ways spirits make their presence known to you, how to interpret their messages, and so much more. While each chapter will provide lots of tried-and-true techniques from my own experience, it is equally important for you to document your own journey. You will discover new things about yourself and your capabilities. You will have an easier time gauging your progress and homing in on what works best for you if you write it down. I highly recommend you have a journal that is dedicated to your mediumship practice. You don't have to spend a lot of money, but choose something that feels special. You may be familiar with the term *grimoire*, which is a book of spells. Most witches or magical practitioners have grimoires containing personal collections of spells, invocations, and other tips that are taught to them orally or that they learn through practice. Think of your journal as your mediumship grimoire. Each chapter of this book contains journal prompts that will help you get started. If mediumship is one of your callings, you will find that lessons, teachers, and important tidbits of information will begin showing up in your life. Your grimoire will grow into a valuable resource as you record what you learn.

Your mediumship grimoire is also a place to document your personal stories. People are predisposed to learn through story. We see this in the continued importance of ancient texts like the Norse Sagas, the Ramayana, the Bible, and more. This is because they aren't just stories. They contain lessons on faith, magic, culture, history, and morals. Most of my magical teachers are brilliant storytellers. This has heavily influenced my teaching style, and I will share a lot of personal stories to illustrate the lessons contained within this book. Your stories also matter, and I encourage you to write them down. As you document and revisit them, you will discover hidden lessons. A bonus is that most folks love a good ghost story and it's fun to have a repertoire of your own to share!

As we settle in, I would like to tell you a bit about my own journey developing my mediumship skills. I hope that you see parts of yourself in my story and that it will make your ability to connect with the spiritual realm feel more accessible. You will begin documenting your own journey in chapter 1.

MY BACKGROUND

Feeling frozen, scared, and accosted by presences I couldn't see was an ordinary part of my life until 2017. I have possessed the ability to connect with spirits of the dead and the natural world since I was a child, but for the first thirty-plus years of my life, I was not in control of these experiences. I did find ways to put my skills to use. I began reading tarot in 1995 when a friend's sister randomly handed me an old Rider-Waite-Smith deck from the 1970s, simply saying, "Here. I think you would be good at this." I learned the cards well, becoming a professional tarot reader and teacher in 2013. The tarot provided a clear conduit for spirits to speak to me. However, because I was not in the driver's seat, it led to some uncomfortable experiences. In my early days as a professional reader, spirits that were attached to my clients would hang over my shoulders, blaring messages into my inner ear. They were able to do this with abandon because I did not set up any ground rules or boundaries for myself or the person I was reading for. The plus side was that my clients often experienced profound shifts in our readings. I became known for my accuracy in picking up aspects of people's lives that they hadn't divulged and my ability to identify future circumstances. As my reputation became more established, the busier I got. I was hooked on the work. I took every client, every gig, every chance to read I could get. I was high on the experience of becoming skilled at something I loved. I was also a new mother and my identity as a tarot reader gave me something precious that was all my own. In fact, it wasn't until I got pregnant with my son at the age of thirty-six that my psychic abilities came into full strength. While I was undoubtedly sensitive before my pregnancy, my abilities had the strength of a nightlight. After my son was born, they were as strong as sunshine.

My enthusiasm for being a professional tarot reader came with a price. I would come home from a nonstop day of seeing clients feeling an unsettling combination of elated and unmoored. I developed a strange tendency to run fevers the night after a shift, which often became full-blown colds. I vividly remember the night I realized I needed to make changes. It was about three years after I had "gone pro" as a reader and teacher. I spiked a 101-degree fever after a day of reading for nine people. I felt like I was completely outside my own body, and I was sick for days. As a result, I finally listened to my spiritual guides who were gently whispering, "You can't keep doing this."

I scaled back the number of clients I was seeing and began to explore what my gifts were composed of. Yes, I was good at reading tarot, but at the end of the day, tarot is just a tool. I also had some real-world skills like emotional intelligence, attunement to body language, and sensitivity to trauma, thanks to fifteen-plus years of being a professional advocate for victims and survivors of crime. These "mundane" strengths allowed me to build rapport with my clients so they felt safe opening up to me. I also determined I was sensitive to my clients' guides, ancestors, and what appeared to be a spiritual team we all have access to if we are open to it. For me, this was the beginning of a very fundamental lesson in cultivating discernment of where my feelings, thoughts, and experiences end and where the influences of the spirit realm begin. This is something we will discuss at length in later chapters.

As I continued to dissect what I was experiencing, I became aware of how often I was bombarded by spirits who wanted to interact. This was not just happening in client sessions. I noticed spirits everywhere. Some of them would stick to me or follow me. This is referred to as spirit attachment, which can be pretty inconvenient and unwelcome. Spirit attachments can bring about classic haunted house phenomena and they can affect one's moods, dreams, thoughts, and physical body. This is another topic we'll explore later.

As time went on, I developed a passion for connecting with spirits, especially spirits of the human dead. By late 2018, I was practicing spirit communication as frequently as I could without putting my health at risk and began offering mediumship and spirit contact sessions professionally. I had the opportunity to apprentice with

Johannes Björn Gårdbäck, a talented magical practitioner and expert on the Scandinavian folk magic tradition of trolldom. Spirits of the dead are not something to be feared in trolldom. On the contrary, they are a normal part of life. My foundational studies in trolldom, along with the friendships and connections I have made with practitioners of other magical and folk traditions—such as traditional witchcraft, conjure, curanderismo, and more—opened the door to working with spirits of the dead as well as saints, deities, plant spirits, and everything in between.

This foundation is what led me to develop the techniques you will learn in this book. I hope the lessons contained here will expand your horizons and inspire curiosity in what lies beyond the veil. As you practice and experiment with the techniques in the coming chapters, you will have experiences that may forever change how you interact with the world around you.

CHAPTER 1
YOUR MEDIUMSHIP JOURNEY

In this chapter, you will have the opportunity to explore your conscious and unconscious motivations for connecting with the spirit world, assess your current belief systems, and begin connecting with the most easily accessible spirits—your ancestors. More specifically, ancestors who can walk with you as you evolve as a medium.

I encourage you to set the intention that learning mediumship is a sacred art. Legends are told of people who can speak with the spirit world. Training our minds is crucial in developing our mediumship skills, so we will begin with a meditation that includes something called a mind room. A mind room is a mental space you create to gain insight into a variety of issues and situations.[1] Mind rooms can be adapted for many uses, and we will experiment with them several times throughout this book. Meditations such as this are helpful because they allow your subconscious to bring forward information that your rational mind may hold back. I encourage you to set aside thirty minutes or more for this foundational meditation.

MEDITATION FOR CONNECTING WITH YOUR TRUE MEDIUMSHIP MOTIVATIONS

Grab your mediumship grimoire and something to write with. Set the mood however you like. You may choose to have something delicious to sip on. You may wish to have a candle or some incense burning. Even opening a window and allowing a cool breeze to come into the

---

1. I first learned about mind rooms from Johannes Björn Gårdbäck. He taught me you can come up with a mind room practice for just about anything.

room may feel lovely. If you are someone who struggles with meditation, give yourself a high five for trying something new. Remember that the goal is practice, not perfection. Be nice to yourself if the meditations in this book are challenging for you, but commit to revisiting them. I promise that the more you practice, the easier they will become.

Take three or four slow, deep breaths. Mentally scan your body, taking note of how you feel without trying to change it.

In your mind, picture a door. Tell yourself that behind the door is the truth about why you feel called to speak with spirits. Before you go through the door, ask if there is anything you need before you go in. Does anything materialize in your hands or nearby? Don't question, judge, or try to change it. Simply notice and accept it.

Go through the door when you are ready. What do you see, feel, sense, taste, or hear? What does the space look like? Are there any other beings there? If so, what are they like? You may find it helpful to state your intention again: *In this room is the truth about why I feel called to speak with spirits.* Expand on this if necessary. Ask aloud if there is anything you need to know as you begin practicing mediumship. What changes?

Take stock of the space around you. Do you like it there? Is there anything that would make it more pleasant? If so, use your imagination to change the space. If anything materialized prior to entering this space, see if you can find a use for it.

Once you feel ready, leave through the door you entered from. Take three or four vigorous breaths, making a whooshing noise on the exhale. Stretch, stamp your feet, and shake your hands to fully come back to your body.

Now grab your grimoire. Write down everything about the experience that feels notable. Now that your subconscious has had a chance to bring up what it deems important, allow your conscious mind to take the wheel. Freewrite about the experiences you've had with spirits or the paranormal up until this point and what you hope to learn. Some questions that may be helpful to consider:

+ What is your motivation for learning to speak with spirits? This may be different from what you experienced in meditation.
+ What kind of spirits do you believe in? Ghosts, fairies, angels, demons, or others?
+ Have you connected with spirits before? If so, what have you enjoyed about those encounters?
+ Have there been times you felt uncomfortable, angry, or scared because of interactions with spirits?
+ What do you want future interactions to be like?

This is your origin story. Revisit it as you practice the techniques in this book. You will be amazed by how much you grow. You may also find it helpful to revisit this opening meditation periodically. You will likely find that the motivations and experiences within your mind room evolve in interesting ways.

ASSESSMENT OF YOUR CURRENT BELIEF SYSTEM

The spiritual belief systems we hold, are raised with, or are otherwise exposed to greatly influence how we view the spirit world. You may find it helpful to take stock of your belief systems at the beginning of your mediumship journey. I trust your beliefs will clarify and evolve by the time you have finished this book.

I work with many people who have trauma associated with their spiritual and religious upbringing. Spiritual wounds are some of the hardest to heal, and I want to make clear that the exercises here are no substitute for deep healing work like that which can be found through professional therapy. That said, over the course of this book, we will discuss strategies for unraveling storylines that have been applied to higher spiritual beings so we can connect authentically without confinement.

Please journal in your grimoire on the following:

+ Describe your spiritual background.
+ Did you grow up in a religious or spiritual tradition?
+ How do you feel about your spiritual or religious background or upbringing now? What, if anything, has changed for you?
+ Is there anything in the meditation and journaling exercise you did in the previous section that overlaps with your current beliefs or spiritual upbringing? This can be positive, negative, or neutral.

This set of journal prompts may be helpful to revisit periodically as your beliefs clarify and evolve.

COMMUNICATING WITH YOUR ANCESTORS

Ancestor veneration is the foundation of many magical traditions. Your ancestors are your fiercest protectors and your most willing helpers in the spirit realm. Some of the most accessible spirits to communicate with are those within your own ancestral line, and this is where we will begin.

There is a renowned interest in understanding our own ancestry and the history that resides in our blood and bones. Advances in DNA technology have led millions of people to better understand who they are and where they come from. That said, this is a fraught topic for many due to varying levels of shame and trauma in our family lines. People who are adopted may also struggle with this topic if they do not have information about their birth families or cultures of origin. Please remember that even if you don't know your ancestors, *they know you.*

I find that people either glorify their ancestry, ignoring genera-tional patterns that may need to change, or they focus exclusively on the negative aspects of their lineage. The reality is far more complex. Our ancestral lines are full of love stories, joys, traditions, and cul-tural practices, which is something we often forget about. It is pos-sible that this chapter may trigger uncomfortable feelings in some readers. Please take care of yourself while also examining the "why" behind any difficult emotions you experience.

ESTABLISHING ANCESTRAL CONNECTION

The foundational practices contained here will allow you to start communicating with your ancestors right away and will prepare you for the spirit communication techniques we will explore in later chapters.

The Ancestor Altar

The first step I recommend to anyone wanting to learn mediumship is to create a simple ancestor altar. An ancestor altar is a place you can turn to for comfort or to seek advice and assistance. You do not need a lot of room, but pick a spot that can be dedicated for this purpose in the heart of your home—the place where your loved ones tend to gather. My ancestor altar is on a small shelf in my living room, close to our couches and fireplace, which allows my ancestors to feel part of our family gatherings. Do not place your ancestor altar in a bedroom. You don't want your family to be part of any intimate moments.

All you need to create a simple ancestor altar is a glass of water, a candle, and a couple of small dishes for food and drink offerings.

The water acts as a conduit for spirits, but it is also intended as an offering that can refresh the spirits after their journey to this physical realm. The candle helps light their way and brings the spirits some energy. It's polite to offer beverages and snacks to someone when they visit your home, so treat your ancestors with the same courtesy. Give them small amounts of food and drinks that they likely would have enjoyed in life or that you would give to any honored guest. Use your discretion and knowledge of your family history as you select your offerings. If alcoholism is a challenge for your family, you may want to offer coffee or tea instead. If someone important to you died of lung cancer, offering tobacco might not be appropriate. Opinions on this topic vary, however. Some believe that it is important to bring your ancestors liquor and other vices because it will keep them from seeking them elsewhere. Decide what works best for your family. Leave the food and drinks out until they no longer look fresh. You will notice when spirits have fed on the offerings. They will look noticeably different. Place the offerings outside, such as under a tree or bush, giving them back to the natural world. Refresh your ancestors' water regularly, washing the glass between each use. I personally enjoy watering my plants, both inside and outside, with the ancestor water.

You can make this ritual as simple or as fancy as you choose. Some people opt to have a small mirror, which can remind the spirits that they have died and are not of this world anymore. Other people choose to have a separate glass of water for each parent's side. I have known people who have as many as twenty glasses for all the different branches of their family. You can set out family photographs or items that were important to your ancestors, but make sure you only include items related to people who have died. You don't want to prematurely call people over to the other side. I personally enjoy giving my ancestors fresh flowers regularly, and I also keep a rose of

Jericho, or resurrection fern, on their altar. Rose of Jericho is used in magical work to "resurrect" anything in your life that needs resurrection. You can also use it to enhance prosperity in all its forms. You can find these plants in many metaphysical shops and botanicas. I use the water from my ancestor altar to nourish the plant while asking for our ancestors to help ensure our family's abundance and prosperity. We ask not just for ourselves, but also for all our descendants to come.

Please do not lose heart if you have limited or no knowledge of your ancestry or cultures of origin. You can have a very active ancestor altar even with no knowledge of your lineage. In addition to a candle and anything else that feels right, set out two glasses of water, one for each parent's side. You may wish to write "ancestors known and unknown" on a piece of paper, perhaps including each family surname you know, and set that on the altar as well. You can give food and drink offerings you would provide to guests in your home. Over time, as you sit at your altar and talk to your ancestors, ask them what they would like. If you take the time to build your relationship and listen to what they have to say, they will share their likes and dislikes. They will also share information about themselves and may even open doors that will enable you to learn more. For those who are adopted, you are not just part of your blood lineage. You are also part of your adopted family's ancestral line. You have double the champions on the other side, so please don't hesitate to venerate the totality of your ancestry.

If you are in a relationship with someone, you may be tempted to have a shared altar. It is generally advised you do not share an altar with a significant other. In my opinion, it is appropriate to do so if you have children with that person because your bloodlines have literally joined. The children will benefit from all their ancestors working together to support them. Although our family altar is contained to a single shelf, it has different areas for my husband's family, my mother's side, and my father's side. We have a son, and I thank our ancestors on both sides every day for their role in bringing our wonderful child into the world.

In our family, animal companions are very important. We also have a spot for our animal familiars who have passed. No one in the family has protested yet, so I suspect the animal lovers in our family outnumber those who may not have cared for family pets. I encourage you to also honor your animal companions who have passed if that feels right to you.

MEDITATION FOR ANCESTRAL CONNECTION

It is staggering to think about the sheer number of ancestors who came before us. When my students or clients struggle with the concept that anyone in their family line looks out for them, I always suggest they do some math. Two parents means four grandparents, eight great-grandparents, sixteen great-great-grandparents, and so on. This gives us a sense of how big our families are on the other side. With that many ancestors, you better believe you have supporters in your corner you couldn't possibly know about. Exercises in later chapters will cover how to communicate with specific spirits. This meditation is designed to help you connect with ancestors who are unknown to you but available to support and protect you as you develop your mediumship skills. We will start with some journaling, so please have your mediumship grimoire available.

Ensure you can be undisturbed for at least thirty minutes. Sit in a comfortable position close to your ancestral altar. Close your eyes and take four deep breaths, releasing any excess energy you are carrying. The goal is to get to a neutral state with no expectations or attachments to what may or may not happen.

When you feel ready, please journal on the following:

* ✦ *What kind of person would be most supportive as you grow your mediumship skills?* You may focus on person-ality traits such as loving, protective, inquisitive, or funny. You may focus on skills or professions such as someone who worked with the dead or someone who served their community as the village witch. You may wish to speak with a scientist or psychologist, which are professions that have a lot to offer our collective understanding of the para-normal. If your mind becomes resistant because you are not aware of anyone in your family who possesses these skills, reconnect with the vastness of your ancestry. Any-thing you need, you likely have an ancestor who has some-thing to offer.

* ✦ *Write one sentence that encompasses the kind of ancestor you are looking for and what you want their help with.* Condensing your wish list to a simple statement will assist you in clarifying what you want. This could be as simple as, "I want to speak with an ancestor who believed in spir-its and ghosts while alive and who can help me learn to safely connect with deceased loved ones." Read your state-ment out loud several times. Make any adjustments that feel right. You will direct your intention by stating this out loud while in meditation. When you are done writing, take three or four slow, deep breaths to reestablish your neutral state of mind.

Envision you are surrounded by a protective circle of light. Any color that comes to your mind is perfect. State out loud, "I am protected. Only that which is for my highest good is welcome."

Set the intention that you want to meet an ancestor who can help you in your mediumship journey. Focus your energy on your intention as you repeat your written statement four times.

Envision a door in front of you. State out loud, "Behind this door is the ancestor I seek."

Go through the door and observe. Does anyone come to greet you? What is the space like? Spirits, particularly those who have not held a human form in a long time, sometimes present as bodies of light or take human appearances they couldn't have possibly held in life. Keep an open mind. If needed, state your intention out loud again.

If someone or something appears, ask them if they are the ancestor you asked to speak with. If they are not, tell them to leave. If they respond affirmatively, ask their name. Then introduce yourself. Have a conversation and ask anything you want. Please remember this can take practice. It may take a few tries before you make contact. If anything makes you feel uncomfortable, tell the source of the discomfort to leave and end your meditation. Always remember, you are encased in that beautiful, protective circle of light. Be strong in your conviction that you are safe.

Enjoy this time with your ancestor. Ask them any questions you have. Tell them about your life, including why you are learning to speak with the spirit realm. Ask them how you can recognize their presence in your everyday life. Do they show you a symbol or color or give you a snippet of a song?

When you are ready, bring things to a close. Thank your ancestor for making the journey to be with you and ask if you can call on them again as you develop your mediumship practice. Ask them to go back to where they were before you called them in. Wait until they are gone, then leave through the door you entered from. Take a few deep breaths as you wiggle your fingers and toes. Check back in with the circle of light you cast at the beginning of your meditation.

Allow yourself to come back to your body fully and allow the circle to gently fall away.

Freewrite on the experience. When you first come out of a deep meditation or journeying experience such as this, your conscious and subconscious mind are working in tandem. Allowing yourself to write without worrying about the mechanics of what you are putting on paper often yields interesting results.

This is meant to be the first step of an ongoing relationship. I encourage you to visit your ancestor using this meditation regularly. How often is up to you, but you may find this is a helpful practice to do weekly until the connection is strong. We will call on this ancestor again in chapter 6.

If this feels daunting, please don't lose heart. Allow me to share a story that illustrates how this can all come together.

Discovering Darda

I was receiving an intuitive reading over video call from a friend of mine who is a very gifted professional medium, intuitive, and tarot reader. Less than five minutes after we began, there was a bang toward the back of her space. She asked if I had heard it, investigated, and immediately said she felt the presence of a spirit whom she believed had made that noise. "Welcome to my world," I told her.

She tuned in to the presence and began channeling messages. She said there was a language barrier, but she believed this person, a woman of intimidating size and stature, was Central or Eastern European, and that she was one of my ancestors. She shared some very specific details that resonated with me. My paternal grandmother was Romanian, and I had been doing some deep healing work with that side of my ancestry. My friend told me this ancestor predated modern country lines, but she seemed to hail from the area now known as Hungary. My friend also said this ancestor wanted to share a meal with me and that if I took the time to connect with her, she would share details that would help me. She was also very specific that I needed to make her some kind of potato dish. She said that the potatoes seemed very important. Challenge accepted!

Over the next few days, I worked on connecting with this spirit. I received the name Darda. I did some research and discovered it is a Hungarian girls' name. It also means "pearl of wisdom" in Hebrew and is the name of a town in Croatia. She told me she lived in a forest along what would be the Hungarian and Romanian border. When I looked at a map, I found a strip of protected old-growth forest that was not only right along the border, but also right outside Peccia, Arad, Romania, where my paternal great-grandparents Stefan and Elisabeth emigrated from.

Darda became more insistent that I get in the kitchen and make a meal—potatoes, as my friend had said. One Sunday, I headed to the kitchen while my son and husband watched cartoons in the living room. I tuned in to Darda and said, "I'm ready! Tell me how to make these potatoes." At first, I was convinced we were making kitchen magic. My hand was guided to smoked paprika, salt, pepper, and thyme … too much thyme, in fact. I was instructed to thinly slice the potatoes and fry them in loads of butter—a delicacy for her, I could tell. The spice mix was heavily applied to the frying potatoes … and then the smell hit me. It was pungent. It was stinky. When the potatoes were tender, they were bitter. "What smells?" yelled my son.

"Where did I go wrong?" I thought. Yet … Darda seemed happy. I suddenly heard an unfamiliar, gentle male voice say in my mind, "It's okay. She was never a very good cook anyway." Laughing, I took a small dish of those stinky potatoes and a cup of coffee to the altar and shared a few bites with Darda. About an hour later, I could have sworn I heard a chorus of more familiar ancestral voices asking if I would please take those potatoes somewhere else.

Do I have 100 percent confirmation that Darda was a real person? I do not. Does it matter to me? It does not. Over time, Darda has become one of my staunchest protectors, and she tends to show up when I start falling back into old habits of playing small and giving up on my dreams. Her presence in my life has helped me make bold choices and give up things that weren't good for me. She is even the one who inspired me to write this book. She isn't a fan of my sharing the stinky potatoes story, but she appreciates being remembered and seen. I know she loves me, and I love her.

As you connect with your ancestors, see if there is information you can validate through research, but I encourage you to not get hung up on needing proof. Developing your mediumship abilities requires a delicate balance of faith and discernment. We will explore this concept at length in future chapters. For now, I hope you have gotten a satisfying taste of the wonder that you will experience as you connect with your ancestors and other spirits.

PROBLEMATIC ANCESTORS

While we all can find support and roots in our ancestry that give us strength and context to our lives, we also have to face the reality that we each have family—living and dead—who have caused harm. This ranges from upholding discriminatory belief systems, to behaving violently or unethically, to perpetuating abuse within families, and so on. However, they are capable of changing and becoming more evolved on the other side. When I talk to spirits who have crossed over, many of them refer to what I can only describe as homework. It seems to involve a reckoning for all the ways they impacted others and their environment during their time on earth. Free will does not appear to dissipate upon release of our human bodies. Some spirits engage more fully in their spiritual evolution than others. This is where we, as living descendants, can help things along for them. For me, changing generational patterns of abuse of women and children within my family line is something I am particularly passionate about. I take time to talk to my ancestors at the altar about my values. I spent a very long time as an advocate for victims and survivors of crime, particularly for women and children who experienced domestic and sexual violence. Advocates must maintain strict confidentiality. Holding these stories was hard on my heart, so I started taking them to my ancestors. Sharing these stories at my altar brought me relief, but I also offered them as a mirror for my own problematic ancestors to reflect on their past actions.

If you feel particularly conflicted about your problematic ancestors, please take time to explore the following questions in your grimoire:

- What is most problematic for you in your lineage?
- What do you want to change for you and your descendants?
- What do you want to change in the world?
- What do you most value?
- How could your ancestors help create the change you want to see in the world?

CHAPTER 2
SPIRITS OF THE DEAD

When most of us think of spirits or hauntings, our minds tend to jump straight to ghosts. More specifically, ghosts who are spirits of the human dead. That is certainly where my gifts and interests gravitate, as can be seen throughout this book. This is where we will start.

Death makes us deeply uncomfortable, yet it is a universal experience. Some of you have likely had the difficult and sacred experience of being with someone as they died. That may even be what led you to this book. Particularly when the passing is prolonged, time seems to bend as the person becomes more disconnected from our physical world. They may begin seeing auras or hearing and seeing loved ones who have passed. Sometimes they will see people they do not know, but who seem to be waiting for them. They may even describe the legendary bright light that appears to be at the end of a tunnel. People who have had near-death experiences often confirm these reports. They are, after all, witnesses to what lies immediately beyond our human existence. Many describe being transported out of their bodies and seeing their physical form as if they were suspended from above. Others have profound reunifications with loved ones and even encounter divine beings such as angels. Upon returning to their bodies, many people find themselves forever changed. There are, of course, logical medical reasons for some of this. As the brain and body fail, delusions and confusion are to be expected. That said, there is more to it than that.

Some comfort with the subject of death is required if you are going to embrace the practice of spirit communication. It's likely that the type of spirit you will most frequently encounter will be that of the human dead. While the following chapters detail some of the other types of spirits you will encounter, the bulk of the lessons within this book are specific to communicating with the ghosts of people. It is impossible to accept that ghosts are real without also facing impossible-to-answer questions such as, "What happens when we die?" It is worth considering some of these challenging topics as you begin developing your mediumship skills. Before we delve deeper, let's discuss some of the questions that will inevitably come up. While no one can provide definitive answers on these topics, I offer my perspective based on my studies and experience.

SOULS, HIGHEST SELVES, AND REINCARNATION

The concept of ghosts is most comfortable when we think of them simply as disembodied versions of who they were in life. For that to happen, however, the innate qualities that make up who we are must transcend the death of our physical bodies. In other words, our soul must somehow survive. We all have at least a general idea of what a soul is, yet it is intangible and, in many ways, indefinable. While much of our personalities, beliefs, and values are linked to how we live and the experiences we are exposed to, each of us has intrinsic qualities we've possessed since our first day on earth. Ask any parent, and they will be able to list at least a few aspects of their children's personalities and tastes that were apparent from the time they were newborns. While talking to spirits is fun and interesting, it is impossible to avoid some of these larger questions, such as what happens to our souls when we die.

Because this is such a difficult topic, I encourage you to do this simple grounding and journaling practice before reading on.

GROUNDING PRACTICE FOR DIFFICULT SUBJECTS

Have your mediumship grimoire within reach. Sit with your feet flat on the floor and your hands upright in your lap. Take two or three slow, deep breaths as you mentally scan how you feel in your body, from the top of your head, down through your toes. Notice how you feel emotionally and the tone of your thoughts. Don't try to change anything. Just observe.

Turn your attention toward the concept of death and what might happen when we die. As you consider death and the afterlife, please journal on the following:

- What thoughts come up as you consider death and the afterlife?
- What sensations do you feel in your body?
- What feelings arise?
- What do you think happens when we die?

Return to your breath. When you are done journaling, come back to your original position with your feet flat on the floor and your hands upright in your lap. Mentally scan your body once more. Are there areas of tension that weren't there before? Are there differences between the quality of your thoughts or emotions between now and when you started?

Take four slow, deep breaths and envision all tension and excess energy leaving your body, drifting far away from you. When you are done, notice how you feel.

Some people are very comfortable with the subject of death, others feel paralyzing anxiety, and most of us fall somewhere between those two states. We can ensure we do not cause ourselves harm as we contemplate these difficult topics by regularly checking in with our body, mind, and emotional state.

THE HIGHEST SELF

You may be familiar with the term *highest self*, which is often used interchangeably with *soul*. However, the concept of the highest self has an added layer. It transcends our physical body and allows our consciousness to exist in multiple dimensions. We can connect to our highest selves through meditation, which often provides a channel for divine insight and information we cannot otherwise access. Our highest self is connected to something bigger than our physical world. It somehow simultaneously exists elsewhere as our human bodies are going about our daily lives.

It is theorized that our highest self is our truest and most evolved self. Even our highest self still has learning and work to do, which is how we end up in places like earth. We touch on this in chapter 3, but it is likely that we have the opportunity to reincarnate. Some believe our highest self will reincarnate many times as we continue to learn lessons that will help our souls evolve. Spirits who remain earthbound, for whatever reason, likely retain definitive aspects of their human personalities because they haven't transitioned to wherever we go between lives. I imagine this place is where we are our most authentic selves, where we remember all the lessons of our previous incarnations, and where we are reconnected with our soul's highest purpose.

An interesting aspect of spirit communication is that it is possible to contact the highest self of someone who is alive, but possibly in a new body. I have found this to be a relatively rare, but fascinating, experience. Occasionally a client will request my help in contacting a deceased loved one, and they report they have come back in another body. The spirit will be able to share details not only about their previous life, but also about their current incarnation. It's intriguing and gives a hint into the depth of the mysteries that await after we leave our bodies.

WHAT HAPPENS WHEN WE DIE?

Let's get the big one out of the way, shall we? You've had the opportunity to journal on your current beliefs, but the truth is that no one knows for sure. I regularly take the opportunity to ask spirits this very question. I have found that, with a few exceptions, spirits tend to be forthcoming about what they have experienced. No two stories are identical, but there are some themes. Many spirits describe a review process where they assess how they impacted others while they were alive. It appears that spirits sometimes drop in on the living during this process, much like Ebeneezer Scrooge and the Ghost of Christmas Past. How long this process takes seems to depend on the spirit and their willingness to engage with the process. Spirits don't seem to have a concept of the length of time that passes in our world after they leave. Many of my clients come to me to contact loved ones who have been gone for less than five years. A consistent message is that, for the spirit, it feels like they just left.

After this review process, many spirits seem to take on jobs or new areas of learning. One of my favorite experiences was with a client who wanted to contact her friend Samantha, who had died of cancer many years prior.[2] Samantha was vibrant and very fun when she was alive. When we connected, Samantha didn't come in to meet us. Instead, she gave us a window into how she was spending her time. She was responsible for "catching" the souls of babies who had died and making sure their homecoming was full of joy and love. Her role also involved sending souls back down to be reborn. My client said, "That sounds exactly like what she would be doing!" Samantha was clearly having a lot of fun, and it was a beautiful thing to witness.

---

2. Name changed for privacy.

Sometimes spirits just get to have a break, particularly if their lives were filled with challenges. Many report going somewhere beautiful, quiet, and peaceful, where they can do simple things that bring them joy until they are ready to take on a new challenge. Spirits also usually show themselves in the form they enjoyed the most. This is not always how the living remember them. My own grandmother made it clear years ago that she didn't appreciate being remembered as an elderly woman. She prefers to present as the pretty, sassy young woman she was in her twenties. Other spirits take on appearances that looked nothing like they did in their most recent life. In the end, appearances are just window dressing!

DOES HELL EXIST?

You may be wondering what happens for people who caused harm when they were alive. Evil entities do exist and must therefore come from somewhere. However, I have not seen anything that matches the Christian description of hell. From what I have observed, even the spirits of people who have committed horrific acts go through the same review process we all do. They have the opportunity to take accountability for the harm they caused in life. Their willingness to do so seems to impact the options that are available to them. I am reminded of the famous quote in Jean-Paul Sartre's play *No Exit*: "Hell is other people." If unwilling spirits are required to face the consequences of the harm they caused and are unable to move forward until they do so…I can see how that could feel like its own version of hell.

WHY DO SPIRITS OF THE DEAD STICK AROUND?

I want to believe that when I die, I will be ready to cross over to whatever lies beyond our human existence. However, the longer I communicate with spirits of the dead, the more questions I have about the reasons spirits stay. While I have no solid answers, I do have some theories and stories that I offer for your consideration.

Unfinished Business

This is a classic justification for why spirits may still be earthbound. Unfinished business covers a range of situations. It could be related to a traumatic incident, such as the spirit of someone who was murdered. If the crime remains unsolved, they may not want to leave until there is accountability for their death. Sometimes spirits seem resistant to leaving because there is misinformation that needs to be cleared up, such as the cause of their death, or inaccurate information about them is being spread. Unfinished business sounds dire but is frequently benign. For instance, a spirit might not feel comfortable moving on until they know a loved one has made it through an important life stage. Other times, there is a message that needs to be conveyed to a living person.

When my father died unexpectedly, I ran into a psychic in my hometown approximately one week after he passed. She pulled me aside, explaining that she wouldn't normally spring this on someone unexpectedly, but she could clearly see my father. She said he was standing by a door with someone who appeared to be a guide. She told me that my dad was unable to move forward until my mother and I had said goodbye. We had felt his presence since his death, and I would hear him moving through the house at night. She walked me through a simple ritual that would allow my mom and me to say what we needed to. We set time aside to do so the following day. Immediately after completing the process, the phone rang. It set off the answering machine, which still played my dad's voice. The person who called was a nosy and overly involved neighbor who drove him nuts. We had a good laugh and noticed the house felt lighter. I followed up with the psychic, and she confirmed he was no longer present and appeared to have moved on.

We must always remember that the reasons spirits stay are not necessarily ones we can understand. It's possible ghosts have tasks, jobs, responsibilities, and learning to do that require them to stick around our world for a while. The overarching point is that we should never assume a spirit needs to be rescued or our role in interacting with them is to cross them over. Unless they are causing harm to others, spirits should be treated as sovereign beings. We'll discuss this more in chapter 10.

Not Aware They Died

Sometimes spirits are present simply because they are unaware they have died. I have observed this most frequently with people who died in an especially confused state or very suddenly. I once connected with a woman who had Alzheimer's. She remained lost in a fog after dying of this cruel disease that had robbed her of her memories. She died in a hospital and returned to what had been her home. She was confused by the new people she found there. It was upsetting for her and the new residents, who would feel someone standing over them while they slept. Items were periodically knocked off shelves and electronic devices were set off in the night. When asked, she stated she didn't want to be there, but was confused about what to do. After gently explaining that she had died and asking if there was anyone who had preceded her in death whom she wanted to see, she quickly moved on of her own volition. The path forward was right in front of her. She just needed the slightest nudge to see it.

Sometimes it appears the shock of dying causes spirits to become confused for a time. Once while holding a virtual séance, I saw a crisp image of a man. He was walking back and forth behind one of our members, who happened to live near a hospital. For me, people who are recently deceased tend to present in a particularly vivid way. At the risk of sounding crass, this man was clearly freshly dead. He paced and said he was looking for his keys. It appeared he had not yet grasped that he had died. He seemed to be on edge, so we chose to not mention it, trusting that he would likely come to realize his situation on his own. When asked what he needed help with, he said he just wanted to go home. We asked him if he remembered the address and pointed in the general direction of where he had lived. He left, and hopefully whatever awaited him was peaceful. While some might not agree with our decision to not tell him he had died, it didn't feel like the right thing to do. While it is true that he could still be wandering around confused, I find that most spirits figure it out and move on when they are ready.

Coming and Going

A common misconception is that spirits of the dead are confined to a single place. While this may be true in some cases, other spirits are able to move between locations.

My husband and I once lived in a very haunted rental with a spirit who came and went as he pleased. This was well before my abilities matured, and I didn't have the foggiest idea of how to handle situations like this. Within two months of moving in, I began having horrible dreams, usually about conflict with people I love. I would frequently wake up at night to see flashing lights in the hallway outside our bedroom, similar to a camera flash. I convinced myself there had to be a logical reason. But no matter what I did to block out all possible light sources, the flashes continued. The flashing lights were always accompanied by freezing air in front of my face and a horrible feeling like someone who hated me was standing nearby. It seemed like my husband was asleep during these episodes, and I was worried he would say it was my imagination if I told him. He was much more skeptical about these things back then. It turned out he had it worse than I did.

He had to leave town for work for several days, and my dreams took an even nastier turn. I dreamed about conflict, death, and illness. The dreams became increasingly violent, and they came every night. The flashing lights and cold were always waiting for me when I woke up. When my husband returned, I broke down and told him everything. When I started describing the lights, he interrupted to say, "Wait—you see them, too?" We started comparing stories. He shared that he was not only experiencing everything I was, he was also regularly waking up to the sound of someone whispering wordlessly in his ear. This turned him from skeptic to believer very quickly.

There were many other occurrences during this time, including constant, unexplained noises and electrical issues. I consulted with a medium who I hoped could assess what was happening. She came to the house and felt instantly nauseous. She said she felt the presence of a man who came and went as he pleased. She said he was not in the home while she was present, but she could feel him nearby. She perceived that his name was something like Ed and that he had been addicted to alcohol, drugs, or both. She said she would bet other people in the neighborhood had similar stories to ours. She said he had likely experienced homelessness off and on and that he had possibly frozen to death, which would explain the cold. The area we lived in had once been very rough, and this story was plausible. Interestingly, the medium was relatively new in town and was not familiar with the history of many local neighborhoods. This lent credibility to what she perceived. She gave us some steps we could take to appease him that were marginally helpful.

We were thankfully able to buy a home after our lease was up. We moved exactly ten blocks away down the same street. Apparently, this was still on the spirit's wandering route. During our very first night in the new home, I woke up to the same flashing lights and cold. Thankfully, it only happened once.

While the spirit of "Ed" was very unpleasant to be around, I gained a broader perspective of what spirits are capable of. Later in the book, we will talk about ways we can offer spirits jobs or tasks. It is possible to cultivate a relationship with even the surliest spirits and offer them a purpose. A spirit who likes to wander in and out of homes, scaring people and making them uncomfortable, is clearly not contributing anything helpful to the community. Spirits can be encouraged to refocus their energy in a more positive way. For example, if they enjoy scaring people, they might be willing to target those who are breaking into homes, stealing vehicles, or hurting people. They still get their kicks, and they also make the area safer.

Not all spirits who come and go are negative, nor do they all seem to be completely bound to our physical reality. Sometimes it seems like spirits drop by to check in on people and places they love, and they leave once they are satisfied. These types of experiences are what we often work to manifest in mediumship. Conversations with the spirits of people we love can bring immense healing and peace. I imagine many of you have experienced these brief but tender check-ins. They can be announced in a variety of ways, such as smells, sounds, feelings, and more. We'll discuss how to become more aware of these experiences in the chapters that specifically focus on spirit communication.

ANIMAL SPIRITS

Spirits of the dead don't always refer to humans. The spirits of animals are also very much present around us. I have met many people who have lost a beloved furry family member and will feel the comforting presence of them jumping on the bed in the night or find their favorite toy inexplicably near their feet. While the spirits of animals are different from that of humans, their connection to us often remains strong. As you develop your mediumship practice, keep in mind that some spirits you encounter may be those of animals. I once assisted someone in connecting with spirits in their home and kept noticing a small dark shadow near the floor out of the corner of my eye. Years prior, this would have terrified me, but when I took a moment to focus in, I realized it was a cat. The person who lived there confirmed that they frequently heard the *tick-tick-tick* sound of kitty nails on the wood floor at night, when their own cat was curled up in bed with them. This is just factoring in domesticated animals. I imagine the spirits of wild animals in nature are also all around us.

NEXT STEPS

Now that we have discussed spirits of the dead, it's time to consider some of the other kinds of spirits you will likely encounter as you develop your spirit communication skills. Even if you are only reading this book to connect with spirits of the dead, you need background in other types of spirits so you can better assess who and what you are dealing with. Not only will it enrich your mediumship practice and assist you in refining your abilities, but it will also help keep you safe. Spirit communication comes with inherent risk. We cannot know exactly what we are dealing with, no matter how experienced or well-educated we become on this topic. As you will learn, different types of spirits require different interventions, especially when dealing with entities who have never been human. The next three chapters provide an overview of some of the most common spirits you are likely to encounter. While this overview only scratches the surface, my hope is that it sparks your curiosity about what else might exist, and that it provides you with the information you need to better differentiate the types of spirits you will meet.

CHAPTER 3
DEITIES AND HIGHER BEINGS

Protection and assistance from higher beings, whether they are gods, guides, or angels, is very helpful when talking to spirits. Many of you reading this likely have a connection with a higher power already, which will make the concepts in this chapter easily accessible. For others, this may prove more difficult. Many of us experience a crisis of faith at some point in our lives. This is especially true for those of us who gravitate toward the path of witchcraft, folk magic, and the occult. You may be surprised to find mention of some secular deities and religious figures in this chapter. Saints, angels, and other divine figures commonly associated with Christianity in particular are strong parts of many folk magic traditions, which I found both surprising and suspicious early on in my practice. It's worth considering that many of our ancestors had to hide their traditional practices and did so under the guise of Christianity. Over time, such deep fusing occurred that it is difficult to fully unbraid these practices. As with all the information in this book, take what works and leave the rest.

At this point in history, the religions that most of us are raised in fall into the general categories of Christianity and Islam.[3] I grew up with exposure to the former, so that is where most of my examples will stem from. As we grow older, many of us find that these institutions are not a fit for us as individuals. Some of us lose our faith entirely. In fact, the third largest category of religious adherents is

---

3. "The Changing Global Religious Landscape," Pew Research Center, April 5, 2017, https://www.pewforum.org/2017/04/05/the-changing-global-religious-landscape/.

those who are unaffiliated. This includes those who are either atheist or agnostic, the latter of which describes those who believe in some kind of higher power but aren't sure what it is. I certainly fell into the agnostic category for a long time.

I was baptized Episcopalian, which my mother says is like "Catholic without the Latin." I never felt comfortable in churches as a child, and I was grateful my parents did not force me to attend them regularly. However, certain prayers and holy figures offered solace because I developed personal relationships with them. This has been a theme as my spirituality has evolved. It is also the larger premise for this chapter. *Big religion, regardless of the sect, doesn't have ownership over deities or your unique connection to them.*

I always tell my students that if you take the divine out of divination, you are left with something hollow. Some have told me they do not believe they need anything but their highest self. However, even our most evolved self is still human. If we had everything figured out, we wouldn't be here on earth in our current "meat suits." There are times when we simply need a higher power larger than ourselves. That said, I understand the suspicion. I have met far too many people who have been seriously injured by those who claim to have a direct channel to the divine that is inaccessible to the rest of us. This is made worse when institutions protect those who abuse, take significant amounts of money from their members, and leave people feeling small and powerless. It doesn't have to be this way.

DEVELOPING AUTHENTIC AND RESPECTFUL RELATIONSHIPS WITH DIVINE BEINGS

Deities with uncanny similarities and origin stories are found in cultures very different from one another. While this is a by-product of colonialization, migration, and many other social factors, something larger is at play. Joseph Campbell, in the classic *Hero with a Thousand Faces*, describes the important cultural role myths serve and the similarities that can be observed in stories from across the globe. He posited there is a cycle of adventure and transformation that runs through almost all the world's mythic and religious traditions. Now, there is plenty of criticism of Joseph Campbell. Not everyone agrees with his premise that all religious and mythical figures have universal similarities and the same trajectory in their stories. Cultural traditions and stories have distinct differences that should be honored. Campbell was also more interested in the overarching purpose mythology serves, rather than the actual existence of the beings in those stories. Regardless, it's worth considering whether the global presence of deities with similar characteristics and storylines means that they actually existed.

Let's take the Holy Mother as an example. She shows up in cultures across the world with different faces, skin color, styles of dress, and myths of her life circumstances. Yet at her core, she embodies the highest and best of the mother archetype. She is fierce and will come to her children's aid in a heartbeat. She will love us through our worst, yet she will also hold us accountable and guide us toward paths that will help us spiritually evolve. No one explains this more beautifully than Dr. Clarissa Pinkola Estés in her book *Untie the Strong Woman: Blessed Mother's Immaculate Love for the Wild Soul*. Dr. Estés outlines how, while the Holy Mother is linked to the religions of colonizers, she is older than colonization and bigger than any humans who would attempt to erase her.

The most important thing here—and perhaps the most controversial—is that you do not have to ascribe to a set religious doctrine to have a profound personal connection to a higher spiritual being. What is required, however, is authentic connection and awareness of the societal constructs and privileges surrounding your practice.

A significant problem in many spiritual communities is the belief that one can simply pick and choose what works for them while ignoring the communities these deities are historically connected to. Take, for instance, Santa Muerte, a powerful holy being who is becoming more visible. The structure of Catholicism has painted a less-than-flattering picture of Our Lady of Holy Death. However, she is beloved by many, particularly those whom society has abandoned. She will wrap those who are dying, who have addictions, who struggle with living consistently honorable lives, and who are grieving in the warmth of her cloaks without judgment. She reminds us that the shadow of death is as necessary as the light of birth and new life.

I personally turned to her when going through a difficult and dark period of my life at the recommendation of a friend who is a devotee of Santa Muerte. I asked for her help and had a clear vision of her weighing my heart on her scales to determine if my pleas were worthy. Over the coming years, she helped me with not just that situation, but many others. However, she keeps me on my toes to make sure I will work for her—and myself—as hard as she is willing to work for me. She is known for being a particularly outspoken deity. I've found that she clearly and loudly communicates what she likes as offerings, such as flowers, coffee, chocolate, and more. She will let you know if the water on her altar needs changing or if it's time to dust. More importantly, she reminds me that working with her requires honoring and supporting her descendants. This means showing up for causes that support Latinx communities. Additionally, while I do not take requests for pro bono spiritual services from the public, I have a small number of fellow practitioners I accept those referrals from. The people they tend to send my way are often in need of divination and magical assistance because they have experienced violence, and traditional channels for support, such as the justice system, are falling short. These are overwhelmingly situations affecting women and children and often members of BIPOC communities. When I commit to supporting these individuals, I do so in Santa Muerte's name.

When you hear the call of a deity, it is important to take note. They reach out to us for a reason. Learn about where they come from and the people who kept them alive. This includes taking the time to educate yourself about the current struggles of their descendants. Learn about their holy days and traditional ways to honor them. Simultaneously take stock of why they came to you and what you feel when in their presence. What do you need help with? What do they need your help with? Build your connection, your devotion, and your practice around this. It is best to do this quietly. Your altars and your practice don't need to be in your social media feeds, particularly if you are working with deities who are outside your own culture.

TYPES OF DIVINE BEINGS

One could fill a library with books on divine beings. For our purposes, the following is a broad overview of deities, angels, saints, and highest spiritual guides. Learning to work with these higher beings will prove helpful as you develop your spirit communication practice. While many of the other types of spirits described in this book are ones we can expect to encounter at one point or another, divine beings require a more proactive approach. As I have mentioned, deities will often reach out to us, but we must answer the call and pursue the relationship.

Deities

Deities are defined by their immortality and divinity. They have never been human and, in theory, they never die. Much like fairies in *Peter Pan*, we can speculate whether deities cease to exist if no one remembers them, but we'll leave that thought experiment for another day. In my experience, deities will reach out to those in need of their support. They will show up repeatedly as one goes about their day. People will mention them randomly in conversation, or you will repeatedly encounter stories, snippets of songs, or passages in books that mention their name. When this happens, it pays to take note. When deities make themselves known, talk to them. Learn about their history and the people who revered them. If it feels appropriate, make them a small altar in or outside your home. You can bring them traditional offerings as well as things they request directly from you.

For example, early in my magical journey, I found myself surrounded by devotees of Lady Hekate, an ancient goddess of magic, liminal spaces, crossroads, and the underworld. She is typically shown as a triple-faced goddess flanked by dogs. I knew very little about her, yet I began dreaming of her. Then I began hearing her speak to me in meditation, telling me to get serious about my spiritual journey. I tried to ignore her.

One day while trying to take a nap, I had a sudden vision of her that jolted me awake. She literally yelled in my head, telling me I needed to speak with a particular friend who was a serious devotee at the time. I sucked up my nerve and texted my friend, explaining that "I thought Lady Hekate was yelling at me" and asking for advice on how to start learning about her. My friend took it in stride. I soon had a small pile of books about Lady Hekate's origins, the people who worshiped her, traditional offerings, and the symbols associated with her, such as crossroads, keys, and a specific labyrinth called Hekate's Wheel. I also learned about the dark and unpleasant ways she had been honored, specifically the sacrifice of dogs and puppies at various points in history. That certainly didn't sit well with me. Sometimes the old ways die for a reason.

While it was helpful to learn Hekate's history, I spent even more time listening to and developing a personal connection with her. I found that she liked not only traditional offerings such as garlic and honey, but also tiny baubles and shiny beads. I was a new mother when I began working with her. I was struggling with postpartum depression, exhausted, and utterly overwhelmed. I felt held and safe when I visited her in meditation. Over the years, my relationship with Hekate has grown and evolved. When doing magical work or spirit communication, I ask that she assist me to safely access the liminal spaces I need.

Hekate was one of the first deities I had the honor of developing a direct connection with, but she certainly wasn't the last. There is a wide world of deities out there.

While we can develop reverent relationships with divine beings, we must always remember that they have never been human, and we are as small as insects to them. We must also always stay true to our values and never make an offer or conduct a task that goes against our fundamental beliefs of right and wrong. As much as I love Lady Hekate, had she asked me to sacrifice a puppy, the relationship would have ended then and there.

While deities will often make themselves known to us, there is nothing wrong with seeking them out, depending on our needs. If you are in need of nurturing, an aspect of the Holy Mother may offer the solace you need. If you are engaged in a confrontation and your confidence is lacking, perhaps Thor, a Norse god associated with thunder, war, and strength, will assist you. There is an exercise at the end of this chapter for connecting with divine beings and a reminder of the responsibilities that come with doing so.

Angels

Angels have been so heavily co-opted by Christian religions that many of us who gravitate toward witchier ways discount them entirely. For me, working with angels has been one of the most rewarding aspects of my personal spiritual practice. While deities might require specific offerings, carefully maintained altars, and regular, dedicated devotion, angels are more likely to help humans without an expectation of returned favors. The trick, however, is that they need to be asked.

According to Christianity, there are three hierarchies of angels, each containing three ranks. The highest-ranking angels are Seraphim, Cherubim, and Thrones. The middle hierarchy includes Dominions, Powers, and Authorities. The lowest hierarchy, which means they are closest to the human realm, includes Principalities, Archangels, and Angels. Many angels have been forgotten as their names have been lost over the course of time. In my personal practice, I work with many different angels, depending on my needs. I definitely have my favorites.

In chapter 7, I offer options for casting protected space, which is an important part of preparing to conduct mediumship. It includes invoking cardinal directions, elements, and corresponding archangels. You may find working with them is helpful to you in your spirit communication practice. As I shared earlier in the chapter, I did not grow up with a close connection with any church. I work with these beings as a folk magician, not as a religious scholar. As such, my descriptions are focused on their magical attributes.

A final note: While she/he pronouns are often ascribed to the angels, they transcend gender. I use the pronouns that resonate most strongly with me in my descriptions below. Use the pronouns that feel most appropriate based on your unique relationship with them.

Archangel Raphael—Raphael watches over the east and relates to the element of air. Air is associated with learning, communication, intellect, inspiration, and clear thinking. As such, Raphael is connected with all these attributes. Raphael is a fantastic ally when learning new skills, communicating big ideas, or developing solutions to problems.

Archangel Gabriel—Gabriel watches over the west and relates to the element of water. Water is associated with emotions, intuition, relationships, and the psyche. I have found that Gabriel is a strong protector of children, animals, and those who need nurturing support. If you are having a bad day and want nothing more than to feel loved and supported, Archangel Gabriel is one to call on.

Archangel Michael—Michael is my favorite of the archangels. I find that many other people seem to feel the same way. He is a fierce protector who watches over the south. He is connected to the element of fire. He is a fighter and a demon slayer, and he evokes feelings of passion and courage. If you need a warrior in your corner or a boost of fiery courage, Michael will have your back.

Archangel Uriel—Archangel Uriel is associated with the element of earth and watches over the north. They are associated with the cold of winter. Uriel is known as a lover of music and other earthly, material pleasures. Call on Uriel when you need help grounding or with matters regarding health or wealth.

While working with angels has proven to be powerful in my experience, it's perfectly fine if this doesn't resonate with you. The larger point is to find beings bigger than yourself who can aid you in your times of need, support you in your practice of spirit communication, and help you stay safe.

Saints

Saints were people recognized by Christian-based religions as being so good and virtuous that they were worthy of veneration after death. Some angels are also considered saints, but most of them were humans. They are not deities or immortal beings, but they can be called upon for assistance in similar fashions. A benefit of working with the saints is that they were human at one point. They can empathize with the nuances of our lives in a way deities can't. There are many saints to choose from. The Roman Catholic Church, for example, recognizes over ten thousand.[4] Similar to angels and deities, each saint has their area of influence, whether it be specific issues, afflictions, professions, and more. Working with them is common in many folk magic traditions because we can call on them for protection and support based on the tasks at hand. Once upon a time, it was probably difficult to match the appropriate saint with a given circumstance. Now that we have the internet, all that is required is a browser search combined with some cross-referencing. While the saints can be petitioned at any time, they all have recognized feast days, which are days when each specific saint is honored.

Communication with the dead and other spirits is frowned upon in many religions, yet there are saints who can be petitioned to assist us. The following are a few I have discovered in my studies and who I occasionally call to in my practice. Legends and stories of their lives and who they are most dedicated to vary widely, so I encourage you to research their backstories on your own.

---

4. M. Petruzzello, "Roman Catholic Saints," *Encyclopedia Britannica*, accessed November 29, 2021, https://www.britannica.com/story/roman-catholic-saints-hallowed-from-the-other-side/.

Saint Lucia—As the patron saint of the blind, "Saint Lucy" can be petitioned to help uncloud our vision or to assist us in seeing that which cannot be perceived with our eyes. Saint Lucia's feast day is December 13.

Saint Barbara—This is a saint who protects those who put themselves in danger. Saint Barbara can also be petitioned by those who hold spiritual beliefs that may be judged by the mainstream. She offers protection from lightning and can offer a veil that keeps us hidden from dangerous forces. Saint Barbara's feast day is December 4.

Saint Michael—A spirit so nice, he's named here twice! Saint Michael is the same as Archangel Michael. He is historically recognized as a demon slayer, so he can offer protection when we encounter spirits with malevolent intent. Call to Saint Michael and his army when you need immediate protection and support. Saint Michael's feast day, Michaelmas, is September 29.

Here are other ways you can work with the saints in the context of spirit communication:

+ Identify a personal patron saint who reflects circumstances and needs in your life. Build the relationship and petition them for support as you pursue spirit communication.

+ Identify details about spirits you are communicating with. Research saints who may align with the needs of those spirits and petition them for support.

+ Research saints who were venerated by your ancestors or within your cultures of origin. Incorporate them into your practice as you connect with your family on the other side.

Please journal on the following:

+ What are some ways you can envision working with deities, saints, and angels?

+ Do you have wounds around certain gods, saints, or angels?

+ Is there an entity you would like to connect with? What is it about them that interests you?

Try the following meditation when you are ready. Afterward, consider if there are ways you can adapt it to better suit your needs.

MEDITATION FOR CREATING AUTHENTIC CONNECTION WITH DEITIES, ANGELS, AND SAINTS

Identify who you want to connect with and why. The more specific we are when calling to divine beings for support, the better our outcomes will be.

As beings who have either never been human or whose human experience was a very long time ago, their approaches to fixing problems can be harsh by our standards. Some suggested reasons to connect that pertain to spirit communication are the following:

+ To request their support and protection as you connect with spirits of the dead.

+ To bring peace to restless spirits—for example, if you live in a home haunted by spirits of those who had a certain profession, you can research the patron saints of those workers.

Learn as much as you can about the higher being you wish to connect with. What about this deity, saint, or angel resonates with you? That is the part to focus on, but also take note of the origins of this being. It may be appropriate to make a tithe of some kind that will support this being's descendants if they are not of your own culture.

Set aside at least fifteen minutes of time and ensure that you will not be interrupted. You may find it helpful to light a candle, perhaps in a color commonly associated with the being you wish to connect with. You can also set out small offerings such as herbs, plants, or foods that are traditional offerings or that just feel right to you. I personally like to include a glass of water when communicating with spirits of any kind. Taking time with your setup can serve as both a respectful gesture and a way to get you in the right mindset for spirit communication. However, it is perfectly fine to approach a higher being with nothing but an open heart.

Sit in a comfortable position and take several slow, deep breaths. Allow all excess energy and expectations of what might happen to fall away.

When you feel calm, envision you are surrounded by a beautiful, protective circle of light. Any color that comes to your mind is perfect. Only that which is for your highest good is welcome in this space.

Focus on the higher being you wish to contact. Say their name out loud four times. Ask them to come close to your body and your mind. Feel how much they appreciate your reverence and the time you have taken to recognize them. Feel how much they love you. Notice how the energy around you changes. Notice the feelings in your body. These may be subtle shifts.

Talk to them, ask for their assistance, and offer your sincere prayers. Ask if there is anything they need from you. Ask if they have anything to offer you. This may be an image, a word, a vision, or something else. Enjoy the wonder of being in the presence of something so much larger than yourself. This can be quite an intense experience.

When you are ready to end the conversation, thank them for their presence. You may wish to ask them how you can recognize their presence as you go about your daily life. Ask that they go back to where they were before you called them in. Wait until you feel they have left. Take full nourishing breaths as you tune back in to that beautiful circle of light you created at the beginning. On an exhale, see it fall away. Open your eyes and do something to get back into your body. Stamp your feet, clap your hands, or stretch.

If applicable, extinguish your candle and either place the offerings outside or maintain this space as an altar if you plan to build an ongoing relationship with this being. Remove old food and plants and refresh the water regularly.

The stronger your relationship becomes with these entities, the less setup you will generally require. For example, I have been working with Archangel Michael for so long that I can connect with him and feel his presence within a minute. Other deities, such as Santa Muerte or Lady Hekate, require more time and dedication. I am judicious about when I call to them as I am granted no shortcuts. However, it takes less time than it used to because I am more familiar with how they communicate with me, what they like, and so on.

Building these relationships can take time and dedication, but it is so worthwhile. May this practice bring you authentic connection with the gods, angels, and saints!

SPIRITUAL GUIDES

Spiritual guides are also divine beings, but in a different category than those we've already discussed. By my definition, spirit guides are not humans we have known in this or other lifetimes. While some of them may have been human at one point, they have become ascended masters and teachers. It is my belief that we all have a spiritual team that includes our highest spiritual guides and teachers, our ancestors, and our own highest self. We just need to take the time to quiet our minds, go within, and ask for them to show themselves and tell us how we can recognize them as we go about our days.

One conversation and a book recommendation opened the door to connecting with my own spiritual team. I had done a tarot reading for a friend, and as our conversation progressed, she shared past-life memories of being a little girl on a train during World War II. She told me about a book that described the place we go in between incarnations. The book is Dr. Michael Newton's *Journey of Souls: Case Studies of Life Between Lives*. I immediately found a copy. This book and the exercises within provided a turning point in my magical journey, particularly those that were specific to identifying my personal spiritual team.

Connecting with one's spirit guides is a worthwhile and enriching experience, and there are many excellent resources out there on how to do so. In the meantime, here is a simple mind room meditation to help you get started.

MEDITATION FOR CONNECTING WITH YOUR SPIRIT GUIDES

Ensure you can be undisturbed for at least twenty minutes. Sit or lie down in a position that is comfortable, but not so cozy that you will fall asleep. Close your eyes and take four deep breaths, releasing any excess energy you are carrying. The goal is to get to a neutral state with no expectations or attachments to what may or may not happen.

Envision you are surrounded by a protective circle of light. Any color that comes to your mind is perfect. State out loud, "I am protected. Only that which is for my highest good is welcome." Set the intention that you want to meet your highest spiritual guide.

Envision a door in front of you. State out loud, "Behind this door is my highest spiritual guide."

Go through the door and take stock of what you find. What does it look like? Who or what do you see in there? Keep exploring. How far does it go? Is there anything that would make the room more pleasant, such as more light or cleanliness? Whatever it is, envision it and make it so!

If needed, state out loud that you would like your highest spiritual guide to greet you. What changes? Your guide may appear as a person, an animal, an object, a ball of light, a feeling, or perhaps something else. If someone or something appears, ask them if they are your highest spiritual guide. If they respond in an affirmative manner—it may not be with human words—ask their name. Ask if there is anything they need from you. You may find that something materializes in your hands or nearby. Give it to your guide and enjoy the satisfaction of giving a gift. Ask if your guide has anything to give to you. Accept what is presented with an open heart. Allow the feeling of this offering to permeate your entire being, rippling out from your core beyond the edges of your perception.

Have a conversation and ask anything you want. This is someone who has been with you since before you came into your current body, and this process can feel like getting back lost memories. Make sure to ask how you can recognize your guide in your daily life. I once had a guide turn into a bird with very specific coloring after asking this question. I began finding feathers with that exact same coloring on an almost daily basis for the better part of a year. I still find them to this day.

Don't get discouraged if you don't make contact right away. This can take practice.

If you encounter anything that feels false or wrong, tell the source to leave immediately and bring your meditation to a close.

When you feel you are ready to end the conversation or your guide is beginning to fade away, thank them for speaking with you. Leave through the door you entered from. Take a few deep breaths as you wiggle your fingers and toes. Check back in with the circle of light you cast at the beginning of your meditation. Allow yourself to come back to your body fully and allow the circle to gently fall away.

The more you communicate with your highest spiritual guide, the easier it will become. Adapt this meditation to meet your needs.

Working with deities, angels, and saints is powerful. Cultivating a relationship with your highest spiritual guide is both powerful and personal. Ask for your guide's help in connecting with the spiritual realm. They can assist you in opening lines of communication and help keep you safe—if you learn to hear what they are telling you.

Please journal on the following:

+ How did this spirit guide practice feel?
ı Who or what did you see?
+ Were you given any clues to look for in your daily life? Did you find any signs of your guide in the first week after doing this practice?
+ Are there ways you can adapt this meditation to better suit your needs?

CHAPTER 4
NEGATIVE ENTITIES

Religion, horror movies, paranormal investigation shows, and more have contributed to our collective vision of what negative entities are. Evil entities exist and the ability to discern their presence is crucial to staying safe when practicing mediumship. However, there is nuance. For example, old gods and spirits were often deemed to be evil by those seeking to convert people away from their traditional spiritual practices and beliefs. In my experience, negative entities have a range of impacts. Some are more of a nuisance than anything else, while others can wreak havoc on people's lives. Remaining calm is crucial when interacting with these types of spirits, as is cultivating discernment of where your own feelings, thoughts, and physical sensations end and where the effects of something else begins. This chapter will describe two broad categories of negative entities that you may encounter and discuss the importance of staying grounded and empowered in our dealings with these types of spirits. We'll end with some journaling prompts and a mindfulness technique that can help you begin developing discernment right away.

LOW-ENERGY BEINGS

There is a category of spirits that I refer to as *low-energy beings*. I believe these beings start as spirits of deceased humans who were hateful or cruel people in life and have since gotten lost. They differ from spirits who were simply jerks when they were alive and are now jerks after death. Low-energy beings have forgotten who they were in life and are completely disconnected with their soul's highest purpose. They attach to the living to suck away our joy and vitality. As we've discussed, moving on from our human lives requires account-ability for our actions and the ways we impacted others. Some spirits would rather be stuck in limbo than face that fate, especially if their lives were fueled by anger and they caused significant harm to others. These spirits can become embodiments of the worst kind of darkness.

The good thing about this kind of negative spirit is that they were once human, which means they are somewhat easier to clear or, at the very least, direct elsewhere. These topics are explored in later chapters.

DEMONS

Demon is a word that conjures up so much fear. Ironically, fear is some-thing that demonic entities love and will seek out. There are many categories of infernal spirits, such as incubi, evil angels, and succubi. Demons appear to have hierarchical systems with royalty who command legions of lower-level demons. There are even magical traditions that involve invocation of these spirits to both harm and help. For our purposes, however, the definition of demon is simply a malevolent spirit who has never been human.[5]

Demonic entities are exceptionally skilled at deception. They can appear as benign beings such as the spirits of children or can even mask themselves as angels. It is natural for us to anthropomorphize the spirits we encounter, especially those we interact with on an ongoing basis. If a spirit presents in a childlike fashion, for example, our minds will naturally create a narrative that fits what we are most comfortable with. It's terrifying to think that the disembodied child voice we may hear in the night is something that is only using that voice to

---

5. For those who require additional information about this type of spirit, Michelle Belanger's book *Dictionary of Demons* is a rich, well-cited resource that offers more information than you will hopefully ever need. Full details and citation are included in the Recommended Reading list at the end of this book.

trick us. As I have said before, we can never truly know who or what we are dealing with when we engage with the spirit realm. There is a line that must be danced around when it comes to dark entities. It's crucial that we stay calm and open-minded, but we also can't blindly trust that everything we encounter is what it initially appears to be.

The best way we can identify whether a spirit may fall into the demonic category is through keen awareness. Even the most cunning and clever dark spirits will give signs of their true nature if we pay close attention. While some signs are external, such as unexplained insect infestations or foul odors, others manifest in our own thoughts, feelings, and behavior. Unfortunately, the longer a dark spirit has access to us, the more difficult it becomes for us to recognize and manage the situation on our own. We are better equipped to notice the influences of outside presences if we are highly conscious of changes in our own thoughts, energy, feelings, and physical state when engaging with spirits. We will discuss this at length in chapter 7, but the best prevention is regularly practicing awareness of our own inner and outer state, rigorous spiritual hygiene, intentionally raising our vibration, and protection.

Signs of Demonic Attachment

It is important to remember that on their own, these all could be signs of a mental health crisis or simply bad luck. Always seek practical assistance, such as mental health and medical care, prior to assuming the cause is supernatural. That said, here are some signs of demonic attachment:

+ Physical sensations such as pain, nausea, cold, and headaches, which often come on suddenly, are protracted, and are not linked to a logical source.

+ Mental disruptions such as unexplained confusion, losing time, and sleep problems, both insomnia and sleeping too much.

+ Emotions and personality changes that do not have a logical tie to circumstances in one's life. The person may feel accosted by disturbing thoughts or visions, which can lead to paranoia, anger, and fear.

+ Paranormal activity seems to follow the individual. This may include apparitions, disembodied voices, moving objects, foul odors, and so on.

+ Things keep going wrong no matter how diligent one is in trying to set a positive course.

A story to illustrate some of these examples.[6] A woman named Sarah contacted me about a possible spirit attachment she'd had since she was a teenager. She said the spirit was a woman who chased her in her dreams. A few months later, she set up an appointment with me for a spirit contact session to see if we could find out who this individual was and what she wanted. We were able to make contact with the spirit of a woman who appeared to be in her late thirties. She had difficulty speaking and appeared to have paralysis on one side of her mouth, similar to Bell's Palsy. When I provided Sarah a description of the person I saw, she confirmed this was the woman who chased her in her dreams. This spirit gave the name Moira and made it known that she was very resentful of Sarah, who was an intelligent, charismatic, and pretty young woman. Sarah had a good life, but also had some areas she hoped to improve. Every time she made headway on these goals, the dreams of Moira would

---

6. The client has given permission for this story to be shared. However, some details have been slightly altered to protect her privacy.

start up, and things would begin to sour. Sarah had grown up in a rural area as a teenager. Moira appeared to have also lived on that same land at one point. She was particularly jealous of Sarah's love life and the boyfriends she'd had over the years. When asked if she was willing to move on, Moira said she was. We went through a process that helps willing spirits cross over, and Moira appeared to leave. Prior to closing our session, I asked Sarah to contact me if she came back and told her that I would assist her at no further charge. While Moira had technically left, my gut told me she hadn't gone far. After Sarah and I parted, I saw in my mind the figure of a man ... but he was only wearing that shape. He had a human face, but it looked like a mask. He laughed with a thick, wet voice, and I instantly felt sick to my stomach. I commanded that all spirits and entities leave immediately. I did a thorough cleansing of myself and my space, knowing as I did so that I would hear from Sarah again.

Sarah contacted me about a month later saying that Moira had come back to her dreams. Sarah gave me permission to do the necessary magical work to send Moira away.[7] As I assessed her situation, it became clear that Sarah was experiencing more than just the one spirit attachment.[8] Once again, I experienced the spirit wearing the shape and mask of a man. It simply did not feel human. I concluded this was a malevolent nonhuman entity—by definition, a demon—who was enjoying the process of unraveling Sarah's life whenever things were going well for her.

The process of removing its presence was difficult. My first attempt at removing this entity resulted in complete confusion. I literally forgot what I was doing in the middle of my work. I spaced

---

7. These are advanced techniques that will not be discussed in this book. If you need this type of assistance, please refer to chapter 10.
8. Spirit attachments are just what they sound like—spirits attaching to a person, place, or thing. This is covered more in chapter 9.

out for what I thought was five minutes, but when I looked at the time, forty-five minutes had passed. My next attempt led to vomiting, which was something I had not experienced before. As I worked my way through this situation, I remained vigilant of my own mental, physical, and spiritual state. I was hyperconscious of my responsibility to ensure this being couldn't dig its claws into me or anyone else in my home.

I had to get creative in weakening this spirit to drive it away from not just Sarah, but also Moira. As I looked closer into what was happening, I realized this entity was not just oppressing Sarah, it was also tricking and goading on the spirit of Moira. It told her lies about how Sarah didn't deserve to have good things in her life. It told Moira that Moira was really the one who deserved friends, boyfriends, a family who loved her, and fun adventures. This entity seemed to gain strength from its influence over both women, living and dead.

My final attempt at removing this entity from Sarah—and Moira—was successful. I was not able to convince Moira to cross over, but I was able to move her into a location where she could be happier and away from Sarah. When following up with Sarah, she shared more information about previous spirit activity she had experienced. This included an encounter with what she believed to be a demon when she was traveling abroad. It turned out she has strong natural mediumship abilities, and we spent time discussing ways she could manage her gifts so she would never experience something like this again. Over the coming months, she experienced one final dream about Moira. This time she was able to tell Moira to leave, and Moira complied. The demonic entity tried two times to reattach to her, and both times Sarah recognized what was happening and sent it away. The last time we spoke, she said she believed this situation was, after almost twenty years, complete.

This was one of the trickiest situations I have experienced thus far as a spiritual worker, and I am grateful it ended with a positive outcome. The reality is that negative spirits sometimes come back. Even if they don't, the world is filled with demons, low-energy spirits, and others who are more than happy to try to take their place. Always remember that the most effective way to deflect negative entities is to take care of yourself. People who maintain their physical and mental health to the best of their ability and keep a positive attitude, even when life is challenging, are simply too much work for most negative spirits.

NEGATIVE SPIRIT ATTACHMENTS

Negative entities look for vulnerabilities they can exploit. People with unaddressed trauma, addictions, and uncultivated spiritual gifts, like Sarah, have greater potential for negative spirit attachments. The classic progression that has been noted by demonologists and the Catholic Church, which has a protocol for casting out evil spirits through exorcism, is as follows:

+ *Infestation*—The early signs of a negative entity include typical haunted house activity, such as disembodied voices, objects moving, and objectionable odors. It is theorized that this step begins with some form of invitation, intentional or not, where the person being targeted allows the entity in.

+ *Oppression*—In this stage, the negative entity draws closer and begins to affect the moods and daily lives of their target. Symptoms include nightmares, unexplained anger or depression, or sudden difficulties in relationships or at work.

+ *Obsession*—The symptoms intensify, and the person is unable to function. Their thoughts are altered, and they are unable to differentiate between their thoughts and feelings and the outside influence.
+ *Possession*—The person's consciousness is in the back seat and the entity has taken the wheel.[9]

The earlier this progression can be interrupted, the better. The more vulnerable the person being attacked is, the harder this may be.

PROTECTING YOURSELF FROM NEGATIVE SPIRIT ATTACHMENTS

The information in this book is intended to build on itself, and most of the nitty-gritty information you will need to ensure that you are as safe as possible can be found throughout chapters 7 through 10. That said, there are some steps you can take right away.

Only Practice in a Clear State of Mind

I do not recommend that you practice spirit communication when you are intoxicated. The less clear you are in your brain and body, the more opportunities negative entities have to mess with you. The only exception would be if you are engaging in a culturally specific practice that involves mind-altering substances led by someone with the proper training and initiations for those rites. Even then, ensuring everyone's safety in both mundane and magical spaces is of utmost importance.

Clearheadedness also extends to your emotional state. It is very common to seek out connection with the spirit realm when we are depressed and grieving. This is normal, and spirit communication

---

9. It is worth noting that possession is not considered inherently bad in all religious traditions. In some, it is considered a sacred practice.

can bring immense healing. It is important, however, to ensure that difficult emotions do not cloud our ability to accurately perceive what we are engaging with. The following techniques can assist you in both releasing strong emotions and noticing when you are being influenced by outside forces.

Practicing Mindfulness
Mindfulness allows us to be aware of what we are experiencing in the present moment. Mindfulness also helps us develop discernment of whether our feelings and perceptions are coming from within ourselves or are being influenced by external sources. This is where a wonderful exercise called Touch and Go can come in handy.

TOUCH AND GO MEDITATION
Touch and Go is a mindfulness technique I learned from a therapist and have adapted for use in spirit communication.[10] Strong emotions can overwhelm us, as many sensitive people know all too well. Sadness, anger, and fear can take us over, as can the mixed feelings that arise with complicated situations. For example, when someone we love dies, we may feel generalized anger at the concept of death, sadness because we miss them, guilt for things we left unsaid and undone, and more. We can get lost in our heads and our hearts as we wade through these big emotions. Rather than fight the feelings, we can touch them and let them go.

When you are experiencing a strong emotion, notice that it's happening. Take a few breaths and pause. You may need to interrupt the flow of your thoughts or otherwise stop what you are doing to truly acknowledge what you are experiencing.

---

10. Thank you, Janelle Dirstine, MA, LPC.

Articulate what you are feeling. Some questions to consider:

+ What type of emotion are you experiencing? Is it one dominant emotion? Is it a mix of feelings?
+ How does it feel in your body? For example, does your chest feel tight or does your head hurt?
+ How is this feeling affecting your thoughts?

There is no need to get into the weeds here. Just lightly acknowledge the answers. For example, let's say you stop yourself to practice Touch and Go when you recognize that you are in a really bad mood and everything is irritating you. You may realize you are actually angry and hurt about something a coworker said to you. That anger may trigger tension in your shoulders and a loop of negative thoughts directed at both the coworker and yourself.

Acknowledge the feelings and give them permission to leave. Literally say out loud, "I see you, [name the emotion]. I acknowledge you and you are free to leave." You can expand on this if needed. To build on the previous example, you could say, "I see you, hurt and anger. I see you came from what Billy Joe said at that meeting. I see you, I honor you, and now you are free to leave."

Observe what changes. Take a few breaths and notice if anything shifts.

This practice is so simple that I initially had a hard time believing it would change anything. On the contrary, I experienced profound shifts in my ability to manage my emotions. I often find that within a minute or two, I experience a loosening in my chest. It literally feels like the emotion I was experiencing dissolves. Occasionally, I will find that a new emotion bubbles up that requires another round of Touch and Go. I encourage you to practice this daily until it feels like second nature.

Here's where the adaptation for spirit communication comes in. Once you familiarize yourself with how it feels to Touch and Go with your own emotions, you will notice there are times when the emotions do not leave or the release feels different. Sometimes, it's because the emotions you are experiencing aren't your own. People who are sensitive to the presence of spirits are often also sensitive in other ways. For example, people with strong empathic abilities can soak up the emotions of those around them like a sponge. When you do not experience a release with Touch and Go, it may be that you are being influenced by someone around you, whether living or nonliving.

Negative entities like low-energy beings and demons feed off the energy of the living. They delight in influencing the thoughts, feelings, and deeds of the people they target. If you have a regular practice of recognizing your emotions and letting them go, you are much better positioned to notice if something nasty is affecting you. If you suspect you are being influenced by another, the following mind room meditation may help you identify the culprit.

LOOKOUT ROOM MEDITATION FOR RECOGNIZING THE INFLUENCE OF OTHERS

Be sure to have your mediumship grimoire nearby. Ensure you will be uninterrupted for at least twenty minutes the first time you do this meditation.

Take three or four slow, deep breaths. Allow all excess energy to leave your body.

In your mind, picture a lookout room with a large window. This room will allow you to safely observe anything that is influencing you without being seen. Give your imagination time to create this space fully. Your lookout room may have walls of metal with a big one-sided window, like a scientific observation room. The walls may be made of earth with an impenetrable crystalline window that is like something out of a fairy tale. You do you. Once you have pictured this space, come out of the vision slightly. Recenter yourself by taking a few deep breaths.

Picture a door that will take you into your lookout room. Affirm that behind this door is a safe space that will allow you to observe any and all influences on your thoughts, feelings, actions, and so on. I encourage you to both state your intention out loud and experiment in your phrasing. For example, if you are experiencing irrational anger you suspect is rooted in an external source, you might try stating, "Behind this door is a safe space that will allow me to see the cause of my anger."

You may prefer a more general statement, such as, "Behind this door is a safe space that will allow me to see all negative influences affecting my life."

Before you go through the door, ask if there is anything you need before you go in. Accept anything that materializes.

Go through the door when you are ready. Observe the space you have created and use your imagination to make improvements as needed. If you were presented with something prior to going through the door, see how you can put it to use. Our subconscious always has a reason for the things we are shown in these meditations.

Focus on the window. Once again state your intention. Observe what appears. Do you see people, places, colors, or lights? It may make sense, it may not at first. Notice how you feel as you look out this window. Do your emotions shift? Do the feelings in your body change? Are you experiencing the same emotions that led you to this space, or are they different?

Leave through the door and come back to your body. Take three or four vigorous breaths, making a whooshing noise on the exhale. Stretch, stamp your feet, and shake your hands to fully come back to your body. Write down everything about your experience that feels meaningful in your grimoire. Use the cleansing and protective techniques described in chapter 7 and consult with a skilled practitioner on the most appropriate course of action if needed.

This meditation stops at observation for a reason. You may find you are simply being affected by the presence of exhausting people. That is likely something you can figure out how to manage on your own. However, if you find you are being targeted by a negative entity, it needs to be handled with utmost care. While these situations are rare, they are serious and often require the guidance of knowledgeable spiritual workers. Tips for finding one are provided in chapter 10.

Always remember that simply being alive is one of your greatest advantages when engaging with the spirit realm. This world was built for the living. Stay calm, remember you are strong, and stay safe, my friends.

CHAPTER 5
OTHER ODDITIES AND POSSIBILITIES

While we have established that not all spirits you may encounter are human, we've barely scratched the surface of what could exist. As you develop your skills as a medium, stay open-minded to phenomena such as fairies, egregores, aliens, cryptids, multiple dimensions, and more. There are many subcultures of supernatural enthusiasts out there, but they often work in silos. Even worse, some point fingers at one another for being too fringe or "out there." It's quite possible that we all hold pieces of the same mysterious puzzle, and judgment could be holding us back from learning more about the great mysteries of the universe. It's also a little silly. If we believe in ghosts, angels, and demons, we shouldn't be looking down on those who believe in extraterrestrials and Bigfoot. The goal of this chapter is to help you cultivate curiosity about other kinds of spirits and unexplained phenomena and to consider options for what you can do if you encounter them. This will include a meditation and journal prompts you can utilize when you ultimately encounter something unfamiliar and strange.

CONJURED SPIRITS

Some hauntings are caused by spirits that are manifestations of group consciousness. You may have encountered the terms *egregores*, *tulpas*, or *thoughtforms* before. Essentially, they are all spirits manifested by dedicated, repeated intentions of the living. They can be created purposefully as well as unintentionally. For simplicity's sake, we'll refer to these types of beings as conjured spirits.

Conjured spirits can be created intentionally in several ways. Many magical traditions have methods for creating spirits that are dedicated to specific tasks. For example, spirits can be conjured to draw negative energy from a person. That energy could then be stored and used to either conduct or reverse baneful work. The conjuring of the spirit, and therefore the spirit itself, is intrinsically neither good nor bad. In my experience, the personalities of conjured spirits tend to be two-dimensional. They have their area of responsibility, and nothing should exist outside of that sphere. Conjured spirits should only answer to their maker or the person they have been entrusted to and there should be a method for destroying them should their behavior get out of hand. However, it is likely that a conjured spirit that becomes wily or aggressive wasn't created properly in the first place.

Conjured spirits can also be created intentionally without the use of magic. One of the most famous cases of this is called the Philip Experiment. A small group of people with interest in the paranormal founded the Toronto Society for Psychical Research in 1970. In 1972, they set out to see if they could manifest, communicate with, and document evidence of a completely fabricated spirit. They named him Philip, and one of the members gave him a full backstory. He was an aristocratic Englishman who lived in the 1600s and was in a loveless marriage with a woman from an esteemed family. He fell in love with a Roma woman and gave her a hidden home on his property. His wife found out, and he was too scared to admit the affair. His lover was accused of witchcraft and burned at the stake. Philip committed suicide not long after. For two hours a week for over a year, the group met, meditated, and focused their intentions on communicating with "Philip." It wasn't until they began incorporating Spiritualist methods and working in séance that they got results. You can find videos of their sittings on YouTube. Philip answered questions about his wife, his lover, and other details of his completely fabricated life by tapping once for yes and twice for no, as well as tipping and moving the table the group sat around. However, his personality and his answers were bound by the confines of the story he had been given.[11]

Then there are spirits that are conjured unintentionally by repeated, focused intentions. For example, when enough people visit a place with the expectation that something frightening resides there, it's theorized that that is enough to conjure paranormal activity. This is potentially a factor in paranormal tourism, where famously haunted locations embrace and work to enhance that history. Well-known haunted spaces frequently have unverified folklore associated with them, the creation of which often goes something like this:

+ People have experiences they share with their friends or online.
+ Some of those people are intrigued and go to that same location. They walk in, exuding excitement, fearful anticipation, and preconceived notions of what is there.
+ If they have experiences that feed into that narrative, the story continues to build and become more fully formed.

Some of it could be linked to an intelligent, sentient spirit, but it could also be fully, unintentionally fabricated. That said, the phenomenon itself is real. This is literally the stuff urban legends are made of.

What You Can Do about Them

Conjured spirits can often be eliminated, or at least diminished in strength, by the cleansing techniques described in chapter 9, which

---

11. Iris M. Owen and Margaret Sparrow, *Conjuring Philip: An Adventure in Psychokinesis* (New York: Pocket Book, 1977).

focuses on hauntings of people, places, and things. However, the simplest way to reset a space that is impacted by a negative conjured spirit is to lighten the mood. Get everyone laughing or singing or have a party where the only rule is positivity. Intentionally infusing a space with joy instead of fear over a prolonged period can be enough to clear out a conjured spirit.

TIME SLIPS

Some hauntings could be caused by time slips or time warps. This is where the past, present, and perhaps even future collide. The most common type of time slips appears to be when someone in the present moment encounters a scene from the past in the exact same location. Andrea Perron, who lived with her family in a famously haunted home in Harrisville, Rhode Island, described what appeared to be time slips in her book trilogy *House of Darkness, House of Light*.[12] In one instance, her mother entered a room in their home and was surprised to see a scene in that same room from the past. It was complete with people who seemed just as surprised to see her as she was to see them. The internet is full of accounts from people who claim to have seen and even entered homes, stores, or churches only to discover later that they no longer exist. Speculation of the potential causes of time slips runs the gambit. Some believe they are the result of ley lines, which is a concept originally posited by an amateur archaeologist named Alfred Watkins in 1922 when he found that ancient sites in Britain could be connected in

---

12. The Perron family's experiences were the inspiration behind the movie *The Conjuring*. *House of Darkness, House of Light* is included in the Recommended Reading list at the end of this book.

straight lines on a map.[13] While Watkins believed this was indicative of ancient trade routes, more metaphysically minded people took it a step further. Some believe that ley lines act like energetic superhighways, intersecting and thereby opening portals that allow the continuum of time to change. Others believe they are moments when, for unknown reasons, the limitations of our human mind fall away, and we are able to perceive dimensions other than those that make up our current reality.

What You Can Do about Them

If you encounter a time slip, it's likely you won't realize it until after the fact. The best thing you can do is research the area you had the experience in. For example, if you suspect you experienced a time slip because you saw a building that no longer exists, you may find it helpful to learn about the history of that location. Research property records and talk with people who live in the area. You may be surprised to find you are not the only one experiencing strange activity. You could also see if the area falls on a ley line. Take a map and assess whether the area you had the experience in can be connected in a straight line with sacred sites or other places where strange phenomena have been reported. Lastly, explore the geology of the area. Certain rocks, such as quartz and limestone, are believed to store information, which could trigger activity that is like a scene from a movie on a loop. Bodies of water are also known for amplifying paranormal phenomena. If you find that the area sits on a bed of limestone or there is a lake nearby, these could also be factors in what you experienced.

---

13. Billy Mills, "The Old Straight Track by Alfred Watkins—Walking Through the Past," *The Guardian*, accessed April 16, 2022, https://www.theguardian.com/books/booksblog/2015/aug/20/the-old-straight-track-by-alfred-watkins-walking-through-the-past.

DOPPELGÄNGER

Doppelgänger is a German word that translates to "double-walker" or "double-goer." It typically refers to two people who look alike but are not biologically related. According to a study out of the University of Adelaide, the chances that two people share the same exact facial features is more than one in a trillion.[14] In a paranormal sense, doppelgängers are nonliving spirits who take on the shape of a living person. They are thought to cast no shadow, which is a way one could identify them. Some say doppelgängers will attempt to talk with the living and tell them lies or give bad advice. Others say that to see a doppelgänger spirit is a sign one will soon die. These beings don't appear to be human spirits but may not necessarily be demonic.

What to Do about Them

Not enough is known about doppelgängers to determine whether their intentions are universally malevolent. They could be caused by trickster spirits hoping to get a rise out of who they are mimicking. They could be a singular type of spirit whose sole purpose is to provide a warning of bad omens. They could even be a version of the person from another dimension. We simply don't know what we don't know.

This is a good time to introduce a meditation and journal prompts designed to bring clarity when presented with particularly bizarre or confusing phenomena. This is very similar to the lookout room meditation we practiced in chapter 4. Please feel free to use this exercise anytime you need it.

---

14. Teghan Lucas and Maciej Henneberg, "Are Human Faces Unique? A Metric Approach to Finding Single Individuals without Duplicates in Large Samples," *Forensic Science International* (2015): 257, 10.1016/j.forsciint.2015.09.003.

LOOKOUT ROOM MEDITATION FOR CLARITY

Be sure to have your mediumship grimoire nearby. Ensure you will be uninterrupted for at least ten to fifteen minutes.

Take three or four slow, deep breaths. Allow all excess energy to leave your body.

In your mind, picture a room that will allow you to safely access the information you need to understand why you had this experience and what you need to do about it. As with the lookout room meditation in chapter 4, customize this room in any way you choose. The goal is to feel completely safe in accessing any information you need. For me, I see a round room with thick walls where I can sit comfortably in the dark while a projector plays the information I need on the wall, like a movie. Once you have pictured this space, come out of the vision slightly. Recenter yourself by taking a few deep breaths.

Picture a door that will take you into your lookout room for clarity. Affirm that behind this door is a safe space that will allow you to access any information you need about this experience. State your intention out loud. For example, if you witnessed your own doppelgänger, say, "Behind this door is a safe space that will allow me to see why I saw my doppelgänger and what I need to do about it."

Before you go through the door, ask if there is anything you need. Accept anything that materializes.

Go through the door when you are ready. Observe the space you have created and make improvements as needed. If you were presented with something prior to going through the door, see how you can put it to use.

Ask what you need to know about this experience or why it happened. What changes? As with all the meditations we have done thus far, it may not make sense in the moment, but feel free to ask clarifying questions about what you observe and experience. This is your time and space.

Ask what you need to do after having this experience. Once again, observe what appears. You may find that nothing new occurs. This could be indicative that you don't need to do anything. Sometimes experiences just happen and aren't tied to something larger. Your subconscious may provide you symbolic messages about what you need to do. For example, a mop and a bucket may appear, or you may see an image of yourself cleaning, which could indicate that some cleansing and spiritual hygiene is in order. A sudden vision of a stone tower could indicate the need for fortifying or protective actions. The subconscious often speaks in roundabout ways, which we must then work to interpret.

Leave through the door and come back to your body. Take three or four vigorous breaths, making a whooshing noise on the exhale. Stretch, stamp your feet, and shake your hands to fully come back to your body.

Journal on the following:

+ Based on what you saw in meditation, what is most important about this experience? Why did it happen?
+ What do you need to do now?
+ What would you do if you encountered this experience again?

Please revisit this meditation and the journal prompts anytime you experience something you are struggling to understand or cope with. Never hesitate to reach out to your support system when needed.

ALIENS

People interested in ghosts often don't overlap with those who focus on aliens and unidentified flying objects (UFOs). This is unfortunate because areas that are suspected hotspots for alien abductions and UFO sightings often have what would be considered classic haunting phenomena. One famous example is the occurrences surrounding Skinwalker Ranch, a five-hundred-plus-acre property in the Uintah Basin in Utah. The term *skinwalker* is appropriated from the beliefs of some Southwest Native American tribes and refers to someone with magical abilities who can take on the shape of an animal. There is vast history linked to the indigenous people who called the land home prior to colonization. In modern times, the Ranch and the surrounding area are known for an abundance of strange activity. Sightings of unidentified hovering spacecrafts and mutilated animals and reports of strange animalistic beings have persisted for decades. These are also accompanied by reports of disembodied voices and other unexplained noises, orbs, and shadowy figures—all things that are typically associated with hauntings. Much like Special Agent Fox Mulder in *The X Files*, I want to believe … and I firmly believe that once one opens up to the strange and unusual, the more one can find.

What to Do about Them

If you have encounters with aliens or UFOs, know that you are not alone. There are thousands of people who have also had these experiences. You can talk with other people in the area or research online to see if others have similar reports. If you are struggling with the aftermath of this experience, particularly if you believe you may have experienced abduction, there are even support groups, which you can find by searching online. Please make sure you inquire about the credentials of the people leading these groups. The best support will be provided by people who have professional training and experience in supporting trauma survivors and, ideally, are licensed professional therapists.

CRYPTIDS

Some of the most persistent legends of unexplained phenomena involve cryptids, which are animals or animalistic creatures whose existence has not been proven. They include beings such as Bigfoot, the chupacabra, and Mothman, and marine creatures such as the Loch Ness Monster. While some people believe that these are animals that excel at evasion, others maintain there is a supernatural connection. My own family is a bit obsessed with cryptozoology, particularly with legends of the chupacabra, who was first reported in Puerto Rico. Sightings now stretch across Mexico and the Southern United States. The chupacabra ("goat sucker") is believed to be an alien-animal hybrid that drains its prey of blood, particularly goats, chickens, and cattle. There are some skeptics who believe the chupacabras are simply raggedy dogs and coyotes, while others believe they were left here by alien visitors.

Bigfoot, also called Sasquatch, is another mysterious and controversial figure that overlaps with paranormal phenomena. Bigfoot is described as a large, hairy, humanlike creature that has been primarily sighted in the Northwestern United States and in Canada. Similar beasts with different names have been spotted around the world, such as the yeti of the Himalayan Mountains and the skunk ape of the Southeastern United States. Many people wholeheartedly believe these are flesh-and-blood beings whose existence will eventually be proven, but there are other theories. Some believe that Bigfoot and their relatives are ghosts of Neolithic beings. Others suggest that Sasquatches are multidimensional entities that can travel in time and space. We may never know for sure, but the possibilities are fascinating to consider.

What to Do about Them

If you encounter a being that falls into the category of cryptids, see if you can gain insight both psychically and through research. If it feels right, use the lookout room meditation described earlier in the chapter or try some of the spirit communication strategies described in later chapters. Document everything you can about the experience. Look for footprints, hair, and security camera footage that can help you better understand what you experienced. Research theories from a variety of perspectives and reach out to others who have had similar experiences. Last but not least, be respectful in your quest for more information. If these are peaceful beings that want to stay hidden, respect them as sovereign beings.

ELEMENTAL SPIRITS

Fairies and other types of elemental spirits, which is a catchall category for spirits such as, but certainly not limited to, trolls, sprites, elves, and so on, are ancient and of a much different character than our own. Cultures across the world have folktales about the spirits associated with the land they live on. Many of these stories are quite dark by human standards of right and wrong, such as tales of fairies or trolls leaving one of their children in the place of a human child who is taken and enslaved. While fairy tales are fictional stories, if we trace many of them back far enough, we find that many are rooted in folk beliefs. These beliefs stem from people's experiences. While we shouldn't wholeheartedly believe each old tale we come across, we shouldn't unequivocally discount it either.

TYPES OF ELEMENTAL SPIRITS

The following provides a small sample of elemental spirits. Most come from European folklore and Greek mythology simply because their stories have been widely documented. Legends of spirits in the natural world often exist at the community level and may only be passed down by oral tradition. Later in the chapter, we'll discuss the importance of learning the stories specific to where you live, which are most likely to be held by the people indigenous to that area.

In the Western world, the mythology of elemental spirits has a deep connection to the writings of Paracelsus, an influential sixteenth-century Swiss-German physician, alchemist, and theologist. His travels across the world influenced his view that there are four elements with four types of spirits associated with them. He wrote a piece called *A Book on Nymphs, Sylphs, Pygmies, and Salamanders, and on the Other Spirits*, which was published after he died in 1566. While each culture has stories that should be honored, Paracelsus was the first to categorize elemental spirits in this way. His contributions to our understanding of elemental spirits are undeniable.[15]

The following examples demonstrate the characteristics associated with different elements. Having a basic grasp of these common personality traits of elemental spirits will help you in understanding spirits unique to your region and what to do if you encounter them.

EARTH SPIRITS

There are many kinds of earth spirits. Some live in the ground, such as gnomes and trolls. The classic characteristics of earth spirits that live underground is that they tend to have an appreciation for things like metals, coal, gems, and similar resources. These beings have a particular connection with the industry of mining. Stories about gnomes and trolls depict them as reluctant to be seen by humans and set in their ways. Other earth spirits are the hidden caretakers of

---

15. C. L. Temkin, *Four Treatises of Theophrastus von Hohenheim, Called Paracelsus* (United Kingdom: Johns Hopkins University Press, 1996).

homes and farms, as can be seen in the stories of the tomte in Sweden or the brownies of Scotland. Sometimes these earth spirits are referred to collectively as the Good Folk or Little People. Some of these spirits embody the very earth itself. Many cultures believe that mountains, trees, rocks, and plants have a soul and unique characteristics. This is called animism. Once while hiking in Banff National Park in Canada with my husband, we stopped at a small lake. In the distance, we saw a mountain that had a clear-as-day face of a kindly old man smiling down at us. It was like time stopped while we were there. Even the mosquitoes seemed to stop buzzing while we were in the presence of this literal "mountain man." I have no doubt the mountain itself had a spirit. I am guessing many of you have similar experiences of being in a spot in nature that also has a clear presence and personality.

What to Do about Them

Respecting earth-based spirits begins with respecting the land itself. For example, don't carve your initials into trees, always pick up litter, and so on. If you choose to leave an offering to a land spirit, you can never go wrong with water, which can simply be poured onto the ground. Please remember that the land itself has vast history we only partially understand. We humans have caused significant damage to our planet. When nature is decimated, it deeply affects the associated spirits, and that can impact their interactions with us.

Also be mindful that these types of spirits generally wish to remain unseen, and many stories suggest they are easily offended. Leaving offerings may be appropriate from time to time. For example, it is standard to leave the tomte a meal of rice porridge and ale on Christmas Eve as their yearly salary.

FIRE SPIRITS

Fire can be both life-saving and life-threatening. Many legends of spirits associated with this element, such as fire-breathing dragons or chimera, are no different. The jinn of Arabic and Islamic folklore are said to be created by God from smokeless fire and possess the ability to shape-shift and perform magic that can harm, heal, and everything in-between.[16] The mighty phoenix, a magical bird found in Egyptian mythology, is said to burst into flames and be reborn from the ashes.[17] The humble salamander is another being associated with fire according to Paracelsus and is sometimes attributed with giving humans the gift of fire. There are also spirits associated with the fires we traditionally tend in our homes, such as in the kitchen and our living areas. These "hearth spirits" have similar responsibilities as the tomte and brownies, but their personalities are a bit more hotheaded and prone to take offense if we aren't careful.

What to Do about Them

Respecting spirits associated with fire requires the same attention that should be taken with the element of fire itself. Don't become overly familiar with them and respect their space and autonomy. If you believe you have a hearth spirit in your home, leaving a small meal and glass of ale near your stove or fireplace, if you have one, once or twice per year can be a nice gesture. Leave the offering out before you go to sleep and discard the offerings outside in the morning.

---

16. Robert Lebling, *Legends of the Fire Spirits: Jinn and Genies from Arabia to Zanzibar* (London: I. B. Tauris, 2015), 4.
17. The Editors of *Encyclopedia Britannica*, "Phoenix," *Encyclopedia Britannica*, November 17, 2021, https://www.britannica.com/topic/phoenix-mythologica -bird. Accessed 20 December 2021.

WATER SPIRITS

In magic, water is associated with emotions, the psyche, intuition, and fertility. Water can also be seductive and dangerous. There are many spirits associated with water, and they tend to share these traits. Mami Wata, for example, is a venerated water spirit of the African diaspora who is known for her fierceness as much as she is for her beauty. Popular culture usually depicts mermaids, undines, sirens, and nymphs as beautiful, naked, often half-human women who lure men to their watery graves. The old legends are more complex. For example, in Greek mythology, there were three sirens who were originally the companions of Persephone. They were cursed by her mother, Demeter, after they failed to protect Persephone when she was abducted by Hades and taken to the underworld.[18] Demeter transformed them into half-bird, half-women who sang beautiful, mournful songs that entranced sailors who eventually crashed their ships into the rocks and died. However, the sirens were fated to die if a human heard their singing and made it past them alive, so their options were limited if they wanted to survive.

What to Do about Them

Water spirits require vigilance from humans. They have a unique ability to cloud our minds and our judgment. Water can lull us to sleep and can literally comfort us to death. This is a perfect example of how elemental spirits have different standards of right and wrong. Think of a child who catches a tadpole in a pond and tries to make it a pet. No matter how gentle they are, the tadpole is likely to die. An immortal water spirit may regard, for example, a human in a boat the same way. The human may seem like a plaything, and while the

---

18. The Editors of *Encyclopedia Britannica*, "Siren," *Encyclopedia Britannica*, May 7, 2020, https://www.britannica.com/topic/Siren-Greek-mythology. Accessed 20 December 2021.

spirit may be a bit disappointed when their "pet" dies, they'll likely get over it quickly.

If you encounter a water spirit, respectfully request safety. For example, if you are with a group of people at a lake that seems to have the presence of a water spirit, you can ask the spirit for protection in exchange for an offering, such as a small amount of unwrapped food. Honey or sugar from a packet is a good option because it is sweet and dissolves easily.

AIR SPIRITS

We can't live without air. It is vital, and yet we can't see it or hold it. Air elemental spirits are equally elusive. Some of the most referenced air spirits are sylphs. They are one of the four elemental spirits referenced by Paracelsus in the sixteenth century, but description of their characteristics is vague at best. There are many stories, particularly in Greek mythology, associated with air-related weather phenomena. In the *Odyssey* and the *Iliad*, both by the Greek poet Homer, the winds are governed by four deities. Boreas is the North Wind; Notus is the South Wind; Eurus is the East Wind; and Zephyros is the West Wind. As the winds change, so do the moods of these deities. Their influence is helpful one moment, devastating the next. Some stories of the spirits associated with the wind are less dire, such as the story of Gluscabi and the Wind Eagle from the Abenaki people of the Northeast Woodlands, which is in the area of Maine, US, and Quebec, Canada.[19] This story tells of a boy who discovers that a great Eagle is the source of a persistent wind that keeps him from hunting. He tricks the Eagle into going with him to a faraway

---

19. Lauren Redish and Orrin Lewis, "Gluscabi and the Wind Eagle (Abenaki Northeast Woodlands)," Native Languages of the Americas, accessed January 30, 2022, https://www.angelfire.com/ia2/stories3/wind.html.

mountain, but he discovers that life is less pleasant with no wind to cool and freshen the air. He helps the Eagle home, and he and the Eagle come to an agreement that sometimes it is nice for the wind to blow and sometimes it is nice for it to be still. Again, we see the polarity of an element that can be both helpful and disruptive.

What to Do about Them

If you find yourself in especially windy conditions, it is possible there is a riled-up air spirit involved. You can request safety for yourself and others or for a physical location such as your town, home, garden, and so on. Always give something in exchange. It is believed that air spirits are partial to smoke offerings such as incense and tobacco.

FAIRIES AND ELVES

These spirits don't fit neatly into any of the previous categories. While fairies and elves, collectively referred to as the Fae, may have a connection to the four elements of our planet, many believe they have access to another realm or dimension. There is also overlap among some of the spirits mentioned earlier. For example, brownies, gnomes, and trolls are considered by many to be part of the Fae. While they may have connections to the earth's elements, they also clearly have access to another world that humans can't experience. Many of us have seen rings of toadstools growing in nature, which are often called fairy rings. Stories about the fairy rings vary. Some say they are direct portals to the realm of the Fae. Others say they are caused by fairies dancing. In either case, to step within a fairy ring is said to risk being taken to their world. While this may sound enticing, to be transported to the world of the Fae is to remain there forever.

What to Do about Them

In general, I suggest we give the fairy folk ample space and exercise immense care when interacting with them. We don't know their customs, culture, or nature, and it is unreasonable to expect they will interact or behave similarly to humans.

If you are someone who wants to carefully observe the Fae, you may be able to get a glimpse into their realm by using a hagstone. Hagstones are simply rocks, often found near water, that have a naturally occurring hole in them. Peering through the hole is said to help one see the realms that overlap with our world. You can also make a small hole to peer through by pinching your fingers together. Next time you come across a fairy ring, take a peek from a safe distance.

GENERAL SUGGESTIONS FOR INTERACTING WITH ELEMENTALS

While each elemental has a unique temperament that must be taken into consideration, here are some general rules that most magical practitioners I know tend to follow:

- ✦ Never take something from an elemental or their land without asking. Make sure you receive a sign indicating that you have received permission and leave something in return. This can be as simple as offering a song or poem to the spirit or pouring some water as an offering. For example, you can tell a spirit that you offer a special poem for them, recognizing them above all else, before launching into something as simple as a recitation of "Roses Are Red, Violets Are Blue."
- ✦ Never make a promise to an elemental spirit that you aren't 100 percent certain you can keep. If you have a nice experience with an elemental, don't promise that you'll see them again if you can't ensure you'll be back.

+ If you interact with an elemental spirit, explicitly state that they cannot follow you home. If this boundary isn't made clear, you may find these spirits visit in your dreams or try to gain entrance into your home.

ELEMENTAL SPIRITS IN MODERN TIMES

While it's helpful to have a broad understanding of the types of elemental spirits and their personality traits, being well versed in the brownies of Scotland may not be particularly helpful if you live in rural Wyoming. It is my belief that we need to understand the history of our locality to understand the spirits that reside there. To relate to elemental spirits in modern times, we must start by looking to the past. The following journal prompts help you consider the range of elemental spirits that could be present in your area. The questions are meant to help you work backward toward the oldest history you can find in your area.

Please journal on the following.

Your Current Home

Consider where you live, starting with the age of the structure you call home, and work your way backward.

+ *Was there another building prior to your home?*
+ *What existed before there were any structures?*
+ *What had to happen to the land in order to build your home or other structures?* Perhaps a water source had to be rerouted or a grove of trees was torn up or a section of a mountain was removed. All these actions leave an impact on the spirits that inhabit these spaces. While elemental spirits are adaptable, they may have a well-justified mean streak toward humans if they experienced the loss of their original home.

Settler Influences

Consider the people who impacted the land in this way and the history of how the land was used.

+ *Who were the settlers to the land you live on and where did they come from?* Get specific about the immigration patterns of your area as they may give clues about the types of spirits people may have brought with them. Research the types of spirits that were important to people of those cultures.

+ *What methods did the settlers use to gain access to or ownership of the land?* For example, while many immigrants came to the United States because of persecution, poor treatment by those in power, and lack of opportunity in their home countries, many of them perpetuated the same tragic abuses on indigenous people once they arrived. Again, this leaves an indelible mark on the land and the spirits that were already here.

Indigenous Influences

This leads to a crucial step in understanding the history of your area.

+ *Who were the indigenous people that lived on or migrated through the land? What happened to them over time?* There are many resources online to help you learn who originally inhabited the land you currently live on. This is an important consideration where I live in the United States, which has a devastating history of genocide and forced migration of Native American people. Sadly, this story has been played out in different ways across the world. Learn the history of the people who are indigenous to your area if you are not of that culture yourself. You will learn a more authentic and nuanced story than what has been traditionally documented. This includes stories of indigenous resilience and joy. Visit the websites of the indigenous tribes and communities in your area, which often have a ton of information about their history as well as events that may be open to the public and seek out indigenous authors in your area. There is a wealth of easily accessible information at our fingertips. All we must do is seek it out and ensure that it is coming from authentic sources.

+ *What are the indigenous stories about the spirits that inhabit the area?* The people who have lived in any given area the longest will generally be the best resource for understanding the spirits of the land. Once again, take the time to find storytellers who are from the indigenous communities in your area. Remember that we don't have an unalienable right to this information, especially if we aren't of that culture ourselves. If these kinds of stories are shared with you, treat them as a precious gift.

Geological History of the Land

Last, but certainly not least, consider what the land was like before humans existed. Go back as far as your imagination can stretch.

+ *Did certain dinosaurs and other prehistoric animals roam the area?*
+ *Was it underwater, desert, or forest at one point?*

As you can see, there could be a lot of things at play if you experience paranormal activity in your home that have nothing to do with spirits of the human dead.

WHY BOTHER WITH ELEMENTALS?

When someone contacts me about spirit activity in their home, they usually begin by telling me the age of their house and whether they are aware of anyone who died there. This is helpful information, but as we've established, it's only a tiny part of a much larger story. The hauntings we experience may not be caused by dead humans or be related to a building. Activity may be caused by spirits attached to the land itself.

Spirits that can cause physical disruptions are often referred to as poltergeists, which translates from German to "knocking spirit." It has been my experience that when people experience this type of activity, elemental spirits may actually be the cause. They literally draw sustenance from the elements of the earth, which gives them a power source that may be inaccessible to spirits of the human dead. As such, they have the ability to manifest in stronger ways.

In 2010, my husband and I had our first encounter with a cranky elemental when we lived in a townhouse in the heart of Denver, Colorado, that was plagued with a litany of strange activity. It was built in the 1970s and didn't seem like the kind of place that would be haunted, but it ended up being a very scary place to live. The activity involved broken pipes, unabated bug infestations, and objects that would occasionally fly off shelves in the basement. I invited a local psychic to our home in the hopes that she could determine what was going on. She told me that, among other things, we had a trapped earth spirit—"like a troll"—in our basement that was causing these physical disturbances. She suspected the spirit had lived within a tree that was removed from the area. She said it was now stuck and, understandably, angry. At that point, I had never considered the presence of elemental entities in the heart of a city. It blew my mind to think about how many trapped earth-based spirits there could be as nature is devastated by expanding cities and suburban sprawl.

Before I paint too dire of a picture, we must remember there are spirits that exist happily in the land itself. One only has to let them live in peace to avoid problems.

Another interesting phenomenon is the way some elemental spirits seem to migrate as humans themselves have moved throughout the world. For example, Colorado's history is heavily marked by the gold mining industry. Indigenous tribes such as the Ute, Arapaho, Cheyenne, Kiowa, and Lakota lived and migrated through the Rocky Mountains for centuries. They were forced out of their ancestral homes as prospectors began staking and vehemently guarding mining claims. This alone left deep spiritual imprints on the land itself. If you spend time near any of the original Gold Rush towns, you can feel the imprints for yourself.

Many young men swarmed the Rocky Mountains hoping to get rich. They worked the mines alongside boys as young as eight. Life expectancy for miners was devastatingly low, as can be seen if one walks through nearby cemeteries. The miners were often first-generation Americans, while others were immigrants, primarily from Ireland, England, and Germany.[20] These miners told stories of tommyknockers, which are beings similar to gnomes. It is believed that immigrants from Cornwall brought the legend of the tommyknockers—or perhaps the tommyknockers themselves to the United States. Cornish miners first reported tommyknockers in Pennsylvania coal mines. As the miners migrated, so did the tommyknockers.[21] Some people claim that tommyknockers are the spirits of dead miners who wish ill on living workers. Others credit the

---

20. Encyclopedia Staff, "Colorado Gold Rush," *Colorado Encyclopedia*, accessed December 22, 2021, https://coloradoencyclopedia.org/article/colorado-gold-rush.
21. Deena Bood, "Tommyknockers," Bella Online: The Voice of Women, accessed December 23, 2021, http://www.bellaonline.com/articles/art58728.asp.

tommyknockers with alerting miners to danger … but only if they like you. Tommyknockers had no interest in assisting miners they deemed disrespectful or somehow unworthy.[22] This begs the question of whether *tommyknockers* was simply a familiar name applied to beings that already lived within the earth or if the miners somehow brought their spirits with them. It's possible that as people keep their traditions alive, they also keep their spirits alive.

---

22. You can learn more about the mining industry and the tommyknockers by touring the Hidee Gold Mine outside Central City, Colorado.

CHAPTER 6
SPIRIT COMMUNICATION FUNDAMENTALS

By this point, you've had the opportunity to consider why you want to communicate with spirits and to start by connecting with your ancestors. You have foundational knowledge of types of spirits other than those of the human dead and tips on how to identify them. Now we are ready to get into the nitty-gritty of how to talk to spirits. You will learn how to speak with spirits one-on-one and in groups, as well as all the fun tools you can utilize if you choose. We'll discuss how to handle unanticipated encounters with spirits, the importance of respecting spirits as sovereign beings, and how to conduct oneself in a graveyard. But first, let's cover the fundamentals of spirit communication.

Spirits communicate in different ways. Conversely, we each perceive those messages using different skills. Spirits are always around and frequently communicating. However, if how they "speak" is not congruent with how the living humans around them "hear," it becomes a classic case of missed connections. This chapter covers the following:

+ Different types of mediumship
+ The psychic senses that are used to communicate with the spirit world
+ A meditation to help you identify your strongest psychic senses
+ Suggestions for how to enhance your more subtle senses
+ Interpreting messages and what to do when nothing comes through

TYPES OF MEDIUMSHIP

The following are descriptions of and exploratory material for each type of mediumship.

Mental Mediumship

Most people experience spirit communication through their psychic senses. This is called mental mediumship. You may be wondering about the difference between *psychic* and *medium*. It's a great question as the terms are often inaccurately used interchangeably. *Psychic* refers to the ability to perceive information that cannot be accessed with your five primary senses. Some people are excellent at remote viewing, which allows them to perceive what is in a space that they are not physically in. Other people perceive auras or have a knack for telepathy, which allows them to communicate without speaking or to hear the thoughts of another person. *Mediums*, on the other hand, can perceive and communicate with spirits. While not all psychics are mediums, all mediums have psychic abilities. That is what makes it possible for us to talk to spirits. An example of where the two abilities overlap is in the practice of psychometry. Some people can touch an object and receive information about who owned it and where it came from, which are psychic impressions. However, they may also be able to perceive whether the object has a spirit attached to it. This is where mediumship abilities come in.

We each have a special blend of psychic senses, which are collectively referred to as the clairs. This English prefix stems from the French *clair*, meaning "clear." The six primary clair senses are the following:[23]

---

23. Clairvoyance as a psychic sense is documented as far back as the nineteenth century. The terms for the other clairs are more modern and appear to have been coined in the 1990s or early 2000s.

+ *Claircognizance*—Clear knowing. Details and circumstances that you have no way of knowing are clear to you and can be validated.

. *Clairaudience*—Clear hearing. You acquire information by experiencing sounds that are not connected to what is around you. This is typically experienced as inner voices or sounds as opposed to hearing with your ears.

+ *Clairsentience*—Clear feeling. Information is perceived through feelings that are not connected to your own inner landscape or your physical body. This is often connected to the feelings of other individuals or emotions that are imbued into a space.

+ *Clairvoyance*—Clear seeing. Information is acquired through images of people, places, and events. This is typically experienced in your mind's eye as opposed to being perceived with your physical eyes.

+ *Clairalience*—Clear smelling. Information is acquired through a scent that cannot be connected to something around you. I refer to these as ghost smells.

+ *Clairgustance*—Clear tasting. Similar to clairalience, information is perceived through tastes that are not connected to anything you have consumed.

If you are just beginning your spirit communication journey, you likely aren't sure what psychic senses you possess. The following meditation and journal prompts are meant to help you identify your strongest clair senses.

MEDITATION FOR IDENTIFYING YOUR CLAIR SENSES

This builds on the meditation for ancestral connection you learned in chapter 1. Please have your mediumship grimoire nearby and ensure you can be undisturbed for at least twenty minutes. You may find it helpful to list the clair senses with some journaling space between each sense prior to starting the meditation. Last but not least, you may wish to set out a small offering of food or drink, a glass of water, and a candle to bring your ancestor energy and to show your love and respect.

Assess your current state of being. Sit in a comfortable position, preferably close to your ancestral altar. Please jot down a few notes on the prompts below. This is the baseline you will compare your experiences to later.

- How are you feeling emotionally?
- What thoughts keep rising to the top of your mind?
- How does your body feel?
- What do you taste?
- What do you smell?
- What do you see?

Get to a neutral state. Close your eyes and take four deep breaths, releasing any excess energy you are carrying.

Envision that you are surrounded by a protective circle of light. State out loud, "I am protected. Only that which is for my highest good is welcome."

Picture a door. Behind this door is the ancestor that is helping you on your mediumship journey. Ask if there is anything you need prior to entering. Go through the door when you feel ready and look for your ancestor. If you have been practicing the ancestral connection meditation regularly, the process of connecting should feel much smoother than when you started.

Ask clair-specific questions. Tell your ancestor you are trying to better understand how you hear messages from spirits. Ask them the following questions.

+ *Clairvoyance*—Can you tell me something about yourself by showing me pictures or images?
+ *Clairaudience*—What is a sound you love?
+ *Clairalience*—Can you send me a smell that makes you happy?
+ *Clairsentience*—Can you help me experience how it feels to talk with me?
+ *Clairgustance*—What was your favorite food when you were alive? Can you send me the taste?
+ *Claircognizance*—This one doesn't start with a question. Think about something you feel you know about your ancestor even though they may not have told you. Ask if what you sense is accurate.
+ Lastly, ask them for one piece of information, communicated however is easiest for them, that you can validate.

When you are ready, bring things to a close. Thank your ancestor for visiting you and assisting you with your practice. Ask them to go back to where they were before you called them in. Wait until they are gone, then leave through the door you entered from. Take a few deep breaths as you wiggle your fingers and toes. Check back in with the circle of light you cast at the beginning of your meditation. Come back to your body fully and allow the circle to gently fall away.

Journal on the experience. Notice the differences between what you experienced with each clair, including which gave the strongest impressions. Compare what you experienced in meditation with your baseline state of being. You will likely be able to pinpoint areas where there was a significant change.

I promise that the more you practice, the more aware you will become of where your strengths lie. When I first began taking stock of what I experienced during spirit communication, I found that seeing pictures and hearing clear voices in my mind occurred almost every time. This means that clairvoyance and clairaudience are two of my strongest senses. I also regularly pick up on details in the lives of my clients and the spirits we are contacting without being told, which is an aspect of claircognizance. Sometimes I experience strong physical sensations that help me identify something important for a spirit or my client. It is not uncommon for me to experience things like tightness in my chest or sudden headaches. When I ask clients about these physical sensations, I often receive information about the spirit we are communicating with. Tightness in my chest has indicated death by heart failure. Sudden headache has come up for people who had alcohol addiction, suffered from migraines, or died of an aneurism or brain tumor. These sensations may also reference issues for the living. Tension in the shoulders or in my throat often correlate with stress or anxiety on behalf of my client. Strong emotions such as sudden sadness, giddiness, or even anger can also bubble up as I am relaying messages from spirits. I simply use these sensations as opportunities to ask questions. These are the ways I typically experience clairsentience.

Some of our abilities will be weaker, but they can be strengthened. As you get more comfortable communicating with spirits, you can ask for messages specific to the senses you hope to develop. I only experience clairalience and clairgustance occasionally. Because I would like to strengthen these skills, I find opportunities to ask spirits to send me messages through smells and tastes.

Channeling and Trance Mediumship

Channeling and trance mediumship fall under the umbrella of mental mediumship but merit their own discussion. When we are serving as mediums, particularly for other people who hope to speak with someone who is deceased, we are translators and facilitators. It is our job to relay the messages we receive as accurately as possible. Sometimes serving in this intermediary role requires something called channeling. Channeling is when our autonomous self takes a back seat, allowing the spirit we are connected with to speak through us. The degree to which you open up is completely up to you.

There are varying degrees of channeling. I often think of it as a volume control knob. At its lowest setting, we are simply repeating the messages or impressions we receive. The more we turn up the dial, the more the spirit takes the lead as our consciousness falls into the background. When turned all the way up, it has parallels with possession. The difference is that all parties are willing. This "maximum volume" process is called trance mediumship. As the medium lets their consciousness fall into the background and allows the spirit to take over, they may lose all sense of time. The medium may not even have memories of what transpired after they come back to consciousness, which may need to be initiated by an outside party. Some of the most fascinating examples I have seen are footage of trance mediums Ethel Johnson-Meyers and Sybil Leek. Their names are often overshadowed by that of Hans Holzer, who was a pioneer in parapsychology and one of the first to incorporate mediums in paranormal investigations. While it is difficult to find the raw video on its own, a short-lived show called *The Holzer Files* gained access to Holzer's archives from his daughter in order to reinvestigate some of the locations. It's a good show in its own right and worth it just to see rare videos of such talented mediums.

I personally prefer to have my psychic volume control set in the midrange. In spirit contact sessions with clients, I often find I need to utilize a light trance state to accurately convey the messages I am receiving. I slowly build up and only allow the spirit to speak through me if we have developed rapport and if it feels comfortable. Every situation is different. As you practice the techniques in this book, be aware of what volume works best for you. Grounding and setting boundaries are particularly important steps prior to engaging in trance mediumship because they will keep you safe as you open up. We will cover this at length in the next chapter.

Physical Mediumship

Some people excel at something called physical mediumship. This is when mediums talk to spirits and receive responses such as tapping, moving objects, table tipping, independent voices, or even secreting ectoplasm, although that is exceedingly rare and often debunked. Physical mediumship is often the goal of groups working in séance. It is powerful when everyone can experience the same phenomenon. Some people just have a natural gift for provoking these types of responses. Doors will open, items are knocked from shelves, tapping noises are heard on the walls. It's fascinating! Because this is not an innate talent I possess, I love using paranormal investigation tools that can help bolster my ability to experience external validation of what I perceive with my psychic senses. This is described more in chapter 8.

Some people believe that physical mediumship is more believable than mental mediumship, but it's also a target of scorn. At the height of the Spiritualist religion's popularity, physical mediums frequently—and sometimes rightly—came under attack for fraud. One of the most well-known cases involves the Fox sisters: Leah, Maggie, and Kate. Maggie and Kate became famous physical mediums as children when they were able to produce rappings that were supposedly spirits of the dead attempting to communicate. Their oldest sister, Leah, took it upon herself to put her sisters into the spotlight, convening séances, experiments, and performances in packed theaters. The Fox sisters' fame coincided with and contributed to the peak of Spiritualism's popularity. Maggie ultimately admitted the phenomenon was false and that they produced the rapping noises by cracking their toes. She later recanted her statements, but by that point the damage had been done.

Cynics love to use the Fox sisters as examples of fraudulent mediums, but not everyone believes it was all a hoax. Maggie and Kate were children who experienced intense scrutiny. Maggie was even the victim of an attempted kidnapping at one point by a group of men who took offense to what she and her sister were doing. The sisters clearly fabricated some of the phenomenon. No medium can produce physical phenomena 100 percent of the time. However, it is possible that the sisters were gifted physical mediums who resorted to fraud to live up to the level of fame they had achieved.[24]

INTERPRETING MESSAGES

Communicating with spirits is not as easy as making a phone call. Spirits have to work with our frame of reference to communicate. For example, if we only speak English, an ancestor who spoke Czech may need to communicate through pictures, feelings, smells, and tastes. While this leaves ample room for misinterpretation, our subconscious minds are highly adaptable. You will find that the more you practice, the more you will develop a glossary of symbols, pictures, words, and more that serves as a shortcut for the messages

---

24. I highly recommend the book *Talking to the Dead: Kate and Maggie Fox and the Rise of Spiritualism* by Barbara Weisberg. It provides a compassionate history of Kate and Maggie's life. Details are included in the Recommended Reading list.

spirits work so hard to convey. I encourage you to reserve a section of your mediumship grimoire where you can document these findings.

When messages don't come through easily or what you receive is confusing, allow yourself to take a moment. Accept anything that is coming through as a viable message even if it doesn't make sense to you in the moment. If you get a sudden name or a vision, no matter how strange it may seem, write it down in your grimoire or speak it out loud if you are practicing with other people. You may be surprised how what seems completely ridiculous to you makes total sense to someone else. I often imagine I am offering spirits a database of mental references that allows them to communicate in roundabout ways if they are unable to send messages that are both clear and congruent with my strongest clair senses. I was once doing a mediumship session for a client who wanted to connect with her father. Once we started, I kept getting images of one of my undergraduate professors. When asked who he was, he said he was her dad. I described what the man looked like to my client and it was nothing like her father. When I described his personality, however, we were able to make the connection. The professor I had in college was an incredibly nice, safe, and supportive man. He also had several daughters and was very proud of being a "girl dad." The client's father had a strikingly similar nature. For whatever reason, I couldn't see what her dad looked like in life, which is normally something I am pretty good at. Rather than fight the messages I was receiving in pursuit of something else, I was honest with my client. We were able to work together to make sense of what came through.

These can be uncomfortable moments, especially for professional mediums. You want to deliver the goods when someone is paying you for a specific experience. Always remember that we can go through the process and do our very best, but we can never guarantee exactly what will happen. I am clear about this with everyone I provide mediumship for, and I encourage you to do the same.

This leads into one last important point before we get into how to communicate with spirits. There will be times when you are not able to make contact. There will also be times when you get things wrong. This is part of the process, and it's okay. If you find yourself in a situation where absolutely nothing is coming through, see how you can mix things up. If the lights are all on, see what happens if you switch to candlelight only. I sometimes like to pull up an empty chair next to some food and drink offerings and make an explicit invitation for the spirit to join us. You can make use of personal items like photographs or things that belonged to the individual. In the paranormal investigation world, these are often referred to as trigger objects. Hold them up and ask the spirits to share what they remember about the item. You can ask them to send you messages as pictures, words, smells, or sounds. You could play a song that might have some meaning to the spirit, like one that would have been popular when they were alive or that is in their native language, and see if that elicits a response. You can also use some paranormal investigation tools or strategies, which will be covered in later chapters, such as taking an audio recording on your phone as you ask questions.

Sometimes you may try all these strategies and more and still end up empty-handed. Again, be honest with yourself and the people you are providing mediumship for. It is better to say, "I got nothing," or, "I may have this wrong, but..." than to lie or overstate what you are experiencing. This is especially important if you are providing mediumship for someone who is vulnerable due to grief.

I promise that the more you practice, the more accurate you will become. You will also become more attuned to the subtle ways spirits communicate. While it is true that some of us come into the world with our psychic senses dialed up more than average, everyone has the ability to refine and strengthen their own natural gifts.

CHAPTER 7
SIX STEPS OF SPIRIT COMMUNICATION

This chapter will break down spirit communication into six simple steps. While this is geared toward one-on-one conversations with spirits of your choosing, adaptations for group practice are suggested later. Before we get into the six steps, let's talk about two important topics: protection and boundaries.

PROTECTION

When we practice spirit communication, it is important to take some protective measures. That said, many people approach spiritual protection as though they are encasing themselves in concrete walls. While this is effective at keeping out negativity, it can also block your blessings, guides, and even the very spirits you hope to meet. I encourage you to envision your protective work as something more malleable. By this point, you have practiced several meditations that involve encircling yourself with light, a beautiful space where only that which is for your highest good is welcome. This is a powerful protective practice on its own. We will build on this technique by learning to anchor and ground to the four cardinal directions. You will even have the opportunity to invoke archangels for additional protection if you so choose. I think of this process as surrounding oneself with something akin to a magical mosquito net. Good things can still reach you, but anything that would cause you harm doesn't stand a chance.

Lastly, while most of us think about setting up protection prior to spirit communication, it is also an important part of the sixth and final step of cleansing. Ridding ourselves of energetic gunk, which is described in both this chapter and the next, is only the first step. We always want to make sure we do something that raises our vibration after cleansing. Once we are humming with good energy, then we protect ourselves. We'll cover this more in step 6.

SETTING BOUNDARIES

I encourage you to revisit your mediumship origin story, which you documented following the meditation for connecting with your true mediumship motivations in chapter 1. One of the journal prompts asked you to describe times when encounters with spirits felt uncomfortable or unsafe. Based on this and the experiences you have had since then, what are the lines you don't want crossed? Perhaps it is spirits who stick around when you ask them to leave or who try to follow you home. Maybe you are uncomfortable with foul language or imagery. For me, I do not like being touched. Spirit touches generally feel like a combination of pressure, cold, and the tingly feeling that follows a limb falling asleep. If I am communicating with a spirit unfamiliar to me, like when I am working with clients, I will simply say at the beginning of our session that I do not want to be touched as we have our conversation. List your top one to three boundaries in your mediumship grimoire before practicing the six steps for the first time.

Now that you have an overview of the protective steps outlined here and you have identified some of your most important boundaries, let's get into the nitty-gritty of talking to spirits.

SIX STEPS OF SPIRIT COMMUNICATION

The six steps of spirit communication are discernment, getting to neutral, grounding, calling in and communicating with spirit, releasing, and cleansing.

While this may sound like a lot, it takes very little time as you become more experienced. I promise that the time it takes to properly set up and release your channel with the spirit world is worth it.

I encourage you to take notes in your grimoire each time you have a mediumship session. What you document is up to you, but you may find it helpful to have some consistency. For example:

+ Date, time, and location
+ Details about the spirit you contacted
+ Tools you incorporated
+ Questions asked, answers received, and how those answers manifested
﹒ Other phenomena such as drops in temperature, external noises, electrical issues, and candle flickering
+ Clair senses that were activated

It is helpful to identify who you want to talk to ahead of time, particularly when you are new to mediumship. Start with someone who feels safe. A relative or friend who has moved on or ancestors you have researched are good starting points. If you can, choose someone whose pictures or worldly possessions you have.

Sometimes this is trickier and you just have to work with the information you have access to. For instance, if you are in a space with spirit activity and no one knows who the spirit is or what they want, your intention will need to be more general. We'll discuss this more in step 4.

It is also important to consider what your desired outcome is. Why do you want to talk to this spirit? Is there something you need from them? Do they possibly need something from you? Consider writing a few questions in your mediumship grimoire ahead of time.

Setting the Stage

Set your space prior to starting your practice. At a minimum, tidy up a bit and wipe down the surface you'll be using. It will put you in the right mindset, and some of the tools suggested here have practical applications for the spirits. There are additional tools and recipes suggested in the next chapter. I do not advise using salt in your cleansing as it drives spirits away.

Set out the following:

+ A candle to light the way for the spirit (some people find low lighting more conducive to spirit communication, and you may wish to have candlelight as the only light source)
+ A glass of water, which is offered as both a refreshment and a conduit for spirits
+ A small offering of food and drink
+ If you have them, a picture and/or personal items related to the spirit you wish to contact
+ Your mediumship grimoire and something to write with
+ If you practice any kind of divination like tarot, cartomancy, or bone-throwing, have those tools handy as well

Do your best to ensure you will not be interrupted. It is helpful to budget up to an hour for your practice. Turn off your devices and ask your loved ones and housemates for privacy.

Let's get started!

STEP 1: DISCERNMENT

As we have discussed previously, awareness of your own thoughts, feelings, body, and physical space is crucial to developing your mediumship abilities. Get clear on these so you can notice the subtle shifts that occur when a spirit is trying to make themselves known.

Without judgment or attempts to change anything, take stock of the following:

+ *Your body*—How do you feel from the top of your head down to your toes? What do you taste or smell?
+ *Your thoughts*—Is your mind racing? Are you preoccupied with anything?
+ *Your emotions*—How are you feeling?
+ *Your physical space*—What is the temperature? What is the light like? How does the air feel?

This is your baseline. You may find it helpful to take a few notes in your grimoire so you have something to compare your experiences to later.

STEP 2: GETTING TO NEUTRAL

The energy you carry into your mediumship sessions will influence what you receive. The prospect of talking with spirits can elicit a range of responses. Anticipation, anxiety, fear, and overexcitement can all interfere with your efforts in a variety of ways. If your emotional and energetic state are heightened, you will find it difficult to remain objective about the information you receive. If you start a mediumship session experiencing fear-based emotions, you also run the risk of catching the attention of spirits with negative intentions. It is important to establish a balanced and neutral state prior to calling in the spirits you want to talk to.

The following steps may help you get to neutral:

+ Say out loud or in your mind, "With four breaths I release all excess energy, far away from me."
+ Take the four breaths and notice the difference. If you don't feel a release, repeat until you do.

If this does not work for you, experiment until you find what gets the job done. One of my favorite clients and students once shared that taking four slow breaths caused her anxiety. She found that quickly shaking her head "like an Etch A Sketch" got her to a neutral state much more effectively than what I had suggested.

STEP 3: GROUNDING

As I have said before, opening up to the spirit world comes with inherent risks. This can be mitigated by grounding your energy and calling in protection and support from your spiritual team. This is where some of the lessons from previous chapters come in.

The four cardinal directions of north, east, south, and west are important in folk magic and many other spiritual practices. They correspond to the four stages of life, the four seasons, the four elements, and so much more. By intentionally connecting to each direction, we anchor and protect our energy in a perfect circle. In chapter 3, we discussed four of the archangels and their magical correspondences. These archangels are watchers and protectors of the cardinal directions: Raphael of the east, Michael of the south, Gabriel of the west, and Uriel of the north. When we invoke them, they protect and assist us from that direction and within their areas of responsibility. An example of how to anchor to the four directions is provided in this section. It is your choice whether you invoke the archangels or simply the directions.

You may also find it helpful to envision your energy anchored above and below. Deep in the underworld is where many spirits reside and travel. Connecting above to the heavens keeps you under the loving protection of the ultimate divine being, whether you call them Creator, God, or something else. I personally invoke Lady Hekate when I anchor below because I trust her to guide and protect me when I move through dark and liminal spaces. I call Metatron, an angel of the Seraphim rank credited with being the closest to God, when I connect to the heavens. In the olden days, I would have been deemed a heretic for mixing such beings, but it works for me. I encourage you to experiment and find what serves you best.

The following exercise is meant to immediately follow steps 1 and 2. You can physically face your body to each direction as you invoke it. You can also simply concentrate on the direction. Allow yourself to sink into this experience to your heart's content. If you want to use a fancy wand or staff to point to each direction as you call it, go right ahead. If invoking the archangels is not a fit for you, skip that part. If you want to use herbs or chalk to draw a circle as you cast, do it. Adapt this practice so it feels authentic and powerful to you.

SAMPLE GROUNDING PRACTICE

Focus on the ground beneath your feet. Visualize energetic roots growing from the soles of your feet, anchoring you deep into the earth.

Turn your attention toward the heavens. Envision that you are connected from the top of your head to the heavens and the ultimate divine consciousness.

Say out loud, "I am anchored. As above, so below."

Turn your attention to the east. Say out loud, "I anchor to the East and the direction of the rising sun. The element of air, governing communication, inspiration, clarity, and intellect. I call to Archangel Raphael to assist me and protect me in the East."

Turn your attention to the south. Say out loud, "I anchor to the South and the element of fire, governing passion, courage, and joy. I call to Archangel Michael to assist me and protect me in the South."

Turn your attention to the west. Say out loud, "I anchor to the West and the direction of the setting sun. The element of water, governing emotions, relationships, and the psyche. I call to Archangel Gabriel to assist me and protect me in the West."

Turn your attention to the north. Say out loud, "I anchor to the North and the element of earth, governing health, plants, and resources. I call to Archangel Uriel to assist me and protect me in the North."

Affirm your actions by stating, "I am anchored and protected above and below, in the East, in the South, in the West, and in the North."

Now envision that you are surrounded by a beautiful, protective sphere of light. Any color that comes to mind is perfect. If you can't see images in your mind very clearly, simply imagine what this would look and feel like. You may find it helpful to say out loud, "I surround myself with a beautiful circle of light, creating a protected space where only that which is for my highest good is welcome." You may also wish to invite in your highest spiritual guide and your own highest self. Ask them to support you as you connect with the spirit realm.

Now that you have achieved a neutral state, are grounded, and are protected, it's time to call in the spirits.

STEP 4: TALKING TO SPIRITS

Say the full name and, if you know them, date of birth and date of death of the spirit you wish to speak with. If you do not have a name, state as many specifics as you can, such as, "I wish to speak with the individual I hear walking through this house at night."

Ask them to come close to you and enjoy the refreshments you have offered them. You may have to ask a couple of times. You can also ask that their highest spiritual guide join them to provide them support. Be patient. You will notice when a spirit comes in, but it may be more subtle than you expect. You may also wish to nicely state your boundaries at this time. For example, "Thank you so much for coming to speak with me. Please communicate with me in the way that is easiest for you, but I ask that you do not touch me and that you go home when our conversation is over."

Pay close attention to what transpires around you. Remember to check in with all your clair senses. Does the air and light in your space feel different? Are there new sensations in your body or mind? Do you see, hear, feel, smell, or taste anything that is different than what you were experiencing before? If you do, describe the sensation aloud and ask questions. For instance, your head may suddenly feel tingly or itchy. You can say, "My head feels tingly. Is that you? Are you trying to get my attention?" What happens when you ask these questions? Do you somehow know the answer? Do you hear or see anything new in your mind? Are there new sensations, tastes, or smells that arise? Jot down any experiences or answers you receive in your grimoire.

If you are not experiencing strong or definitive answers through your clair senses, you can ask for external validation. For example, you can say, "I am not sure I am understanding you. If you are here, can you let me know by flickering the candle or knocking on the wall?" You can also ask for the spirit to touch your hand, speak in your ear, or move an object. Remember that it usually takes significant energy for spirits to join us, even for short periods of time. Physical actions like these may not be possible for all spirits.

If spirits claim to be familiar to you, don't take it at face value. Test them a bit. The simplest way is to ask them what your name is. If a spirit claims to be your grandmother, for example, but can't tell you your full name, they shouldn't be trusted. You can also ask them about memories you share or quiz them a bit on family history. You don't need to turn this into an interrogation. You'll know after a question or two. If you are someone who has particularly strong clairvoyant skills, you can walk around the spirit to see if they are authentic or wearing the mask of the one you called in. If you get any indication that the spirit in your presence isn't the one you invited, firmly state that they must leave and that you claim the space as your own. Keep repeating this statement until you feel them leave. Move on to steps 5 and 6, and try another day.

If the spirit in your presence is the one you called in, enjoy your conversation. Talk to them and take the time to listen. It can be helpful to ask for things you can confirm. There are few things more satisfying than getting information during a mediumship session you can later verify.

If you are struggling to get clear messages and you have divination tools handy, ask the spirit to speak to you through your tarot cards, and so on. For example, you can ask the spirit a question and pull a card to help divine the answer. Take notes on what you experience.

If you get overwhelmed at any point, tell the spirit to pull back a bit. Please also remember that you may not get interaction every time.

STEP 5: RELEASING

Signs you are ready to release include the following:

+ You are simply done talking
+ You are beginning to feel weak or tired
+ The spirit is not as engaged

Give your sincere thanks to the spirit and, if you called them, to their spiritual guide. It takes effort for spirits of the dead to engage with the living, so make sure you convey how much you appreciated their visit. When you are ready to say goodbye, state that it is time for them to return to where they were before you called them. State your request again if necessary and wait until you feel them go.

Reconnect with the beautiful circle of light you created at the beginning. On an exhale, see it gently fall away. If you invited your highest spiritual guide and highest self to join you, thank them. Ask them to return to where they were before you called them in. Once again, wait until you feel them depart.

Release your anchors by stating, "I release my connection to the North. I release my connection to the West. I release my connection to the South. I release my connection to the East. I release from above. I release from below." If you invoked the archangels or any other deities, thank them and ask for them to go back to where they were before you called them in.

Reconnect with your body. Take several full breaths. Stand up and stretch or give your limbs a wiggle. Document any additional findings in your grimoire.

Snuff out the candle and place the offerings of food, water, and other drinks somewhere outside, such as under a tree or bush. You can also treat the space as an altar if that feels right. Replenish the water and bring the food and drinks outside once they are no longer fresh. Maintaining the space will help if you want to build an ongoing relationship with that particular spirit.

STEP 6: CLEANSE, RAISE YOUR VIBE, AND PROTECT

Every mediumship session will leave a degree of spiritual residue that should be addressed immediately. Energetic hygiene is paramount to maintaining a healthy spiritual practice. Our sixth and final step consists of three parts:

+ Cleansing yourself and your space
+ Raising your vibration to a high level
+ Protecting your energy

The following is focused on tool-free methods. It's important to develop techniques that do not require anything other than your own intentions. It will help you build your psychic strength and will also ensure that you are never dependent on something external. That said, there are fantastic ingredients, tools, and products that you can use as reinforcements to bolster your efforts. These are discussed further in the next chapter in addition to some simple "around the house" folk magic recipes you can incorporate into your practice.

Cleansing Yourself and Your Space

The simplest, tool-free method for energetically cleansing yourself is to visualize bright light flooding through your body, washing away any spiritual gunk. You can then extend that vision to include bright light flooding your space.

I am partial to following this visualization with a few spritzes of Florida water in my space and on my person. Florida water is technically a cologne that was created by the company Murray & Lanman in the nineteenth century. It has a long history of magical use, particularly for spiritual cleansing, blessing, and protecting. There are lovely Florida water blends made by independent magical practitioners and you can even make your own. Recipes differ, but the base always includes orange and clove with a variety of flowers and herbs. Salt is another powerful cleanser, which we'll talk more about in chapter 7. A simple salt scrub or salt bath can also help cleanse your spirit. Find what works for you. Just don't neglect your spiritual hygiene.

Raising Your Vibe

You are like an empty vessel after you rid yourself of spiritual gunk. It's important to fill up that space with something positive. This is often a neglected step. If we don't intentionally fill empty space with something desirable, we'll pick up energetic debris as we go about our day. The simplest thing you can do is follow your cleansing with something joyful. You can envision a beloved color emanating from your heart, filling your body and extending out through your home, neighborhood, town, country, world … as far out as you can imagine. You can sing or listen to music and dance. Do whatever fills your spirit and makes you happy and grateful to be alive.

PROTECTION

Now that you have raised your vibration, it's time to protect it. You can simply envision you are encased in a golden sphere of light. As mentioned previously, you don't want this barrier to be an impenetrable wall. Blessings and goodness can still reach you, but anything negative or low energy will be turned away.

That completes our sixth and final step. The process of developing mediumship abilities is analogous to physical fitness in many ways. If you decide to start running, you don't immediately take on a marathon. It takes time to build endurance and to identify a training method that works for you. Please be patient with yourself as you work to cultivate these skills. Practice these steps, adapt them as necessary, and don't give up. The more you work at this, the stronger you will become.

ADAPTING THE SIX STEPS FOR GROUP PRACTICE

These six steps can easily be adapted for group practice, which is also called séance or sitting. The following description is specific to séances that are conducted in person. However, you don't need to be in the same location to hold a séance. Most of the spirit contact sessions I conduct, whether they are with one other person or a group of ten, are held virtually. Physical distance makes no difference when we sit together in spirit. Some suggestions for safely holding virtual séances are provided later.

FORMING THE GROUP AND
ESTABLISHING YOUR DESIRED OUTCOMES

It is helpful if all participants are open-minded and genuinely excited about the prospect of working together to contact spirits. Nothing cools a séance faster than overt skepticism. The number of people in your séance is up to you. I personally prefer groups of up to ten people.

Group members should discuss ahead of time what they hope to achieve. For example, if one member hopes to reach their great-grandmother and another person wants to invoke a demon, this may not be a great match. Each person can identify who they hope to contact, such as deceased loved ones or ancestors, or the group could decide to focus their intentions on contacting one specific spirit. There are a million ways this could look, but the larger point is to have a shared vision of where you'd like to go before you "get in the car."

DESIGNATE A FACILITATOR

When you work with other people to contact spirits, someone needs to act as the facilitator. Everyone can be involved in communicating with the spirits once the space is set, but it's best if one person takes the lead. The person who holds space for the group will guide everyone through each of the six steps. The facilitator must also be willing to assume responsibility for the group. This includes, but isn't limited to, the following:

- Noticing if others are experiencing distress and responding appropriately. This can be as simple as noticing that a member is crying and silently passing them a tissue or helping the group reestablish their neutral state if members get scared or otherwise adversely emotionally heightened.
- Addressing any dangerous or inappropriate behavior, such as being disrespectful of others, provoking spirits, or going against any established ground rules of the group.
- Bringing the séance to a close.

If you are fortunate enough to have a group that regularly meets to practice, feel free to experiment. Your group may try sharing the responsibility of facilitating the séance or taking turns guiding the group through different steps.

ADAPTING THE SIX STEPS

Traditionally, séances are conducted in low light with members sitting around a table. Hands can be placed on the table with pinky fingers touching, creating an energetic circle among you. Once your group has established a facilitator, they will be responsible for leading everyone through steps 1 through 3, which essentially become a guided meditation.

Once members have practiced discernment, achieved a neutral state, and the circle has been cast, proceed to step 4. It is the group's choice to call to specific spirits, focus on the spirits who just happen to be around, or do a combination of the two. It's okay to loosen up a bit at this point. Séances don't have to be overly serious affairs. In fact, they were historically held for entertainment as much as spiritual enlightenment. Laugh and have some fun! Keeping the vibe lighthearted also helps ensure that only spirits who match your high energy will be welcome.

When it is time to end the séance, the facilitator will guide the group through step 5. It is very important that all members are committed to closing the portal that was opened and that everyone is in agreement that all spirits have left before proceeding. Once this has been achieved, the facilitator should lead the group through the three parts of step 6. Group members should be encouraged to continue their spiritual hygiene upon returning home, taking a salt bath, or using a salt scrub on their feet.

VIRTUAL SÉANCE

Many people think spiritual work needs to be conducted in person to be effective. I get it. I used to hate the idea of seeing clients virtually. I had never tried it, but I convinced myself it couldn't work. Then the pandemic of 2020 began, and connecting remotely became the norm. People in all kinds of professions had the choice of adapting or becoming obsolete. I discovered that seeing clients virtually was wonderful. People could be in their ultimate comfort zone, and it made no difference in the connection we were able to establish. I was also suddenly able to connect with people from across the world. If that's not magic, I don't know what is!

If you want to connect with friends virtually to hold a séance, you can follow the steps listed previously. The primary differences are as follows:

+ Members do not have the reinforcement of physical touch.
+ Everyone is responsible for their own space.

+ Members are responsible for themselves as well as for other people and animals living in the home.

Participating in a séance from your home can stir up paranormal activity, particularly for people who are highly sensitive or who live in a location that is already active. The steps to prepare and release the connection are especially important when you are practicing at home. Prior to your practice, it can be helpful to tell the spirits in your space about the séance. If you aren't sure if you have household spirits, act as if you do. Go room to room and politely say that you'll be working with a group to contact different spirits. If you want them to be involved, this would be a good time to ask. If you do not want them engaged, tell them courteously. You may wish to provide your household spirits a small food or drink offering to thank them for their cooperation. If you have a good relationship with spirits in your home, you can also ask for their assistance in maintaining the peace.

Virtual séances can be powerful and intimate. They lessen accessibility challenges for people who may be unable to travel for these experiences. For some, the ability to participate from their homes brings immense comfort. There are many benefits to connecting this way. However, you are the only one who can decide if those benefits outweigh the risks of stirring up activity in your home. If you live with other people, particularly those who are psychically sensitive or have vulnerabilities such as addictions or unmanaged mental health challenges, participating in séances from home may not be a wise choice. Other people shouldn't have to pay the price if your household spirits become riled up or if the séance isn't closed completely and spirits decide to stick around. As with everything we have discussed, use discretion, make wise choices, and adapt as needed.

In closing, practicing mediumship on your own is powerful. Self-consciousness falls away, which allows for experimentation that may not feel comfortable in the presence of others. That said, many of us are solitary practitioners out of sheer necessity. It's a blessing to share experiences like this with like-minded people. If you are so fortunate as to have others to practice with, I hope it brings you joy.

UNEXPECTED SPIRIT CONTACT

It's all well and good to thoughtfully prepare for a mediumship session, but connections with the spirit world sometimes happen when we least expect them. It is normal and understandable to feel rattled or even scared when a spirit makes their presence known unexpectedly. If we calm our natural physiological responses and come back to the six steps, what starts as an unexpected and perhaps unwelcome intrusion can turn into an interesting visit. Always remember that you are in charge. You make the rules about when and how you will talk to spirits. For example, if you are trying to go to sleep in a hotel room and you feel an invisible hand stroke your hair or hear a disembodied voice while you are trying to take a shower, you have every right to set boundaries and state that you don't want to be bothered.

Most of us get scared or startled when a spirit announces themselves unexpectedly. It's a normal response. Our heart starts beating faster, breathing may become quickened or shallow, and our flight, fright, or freeze response may kick in. Focusing on your breath will help you override these normal physical responses to potential danger. Breathing slowly and deeply will give you space to take stock of your surroundings, your body, your emotions, and your thoughts. Then you can assess if you are truly in danger or simply startled.

ON-THE-FLY GROUNDING AND PROTECTION PRACTICE

Here is a simple, easy-to-memorize practice you can use anytime you find yourself in the presence of spirits unexpectedly.

- *Focus on your breath.* Take slow, deep breaths as you assess what startled you.
- *Anchor below.* Feel all four corners of your feet firmly on the ground. Imagine you have roots anchoring you deep into the earth.
- *Anchor above.* Focus on the top of your head. Imagine a beam of light shooting from the top of your head into the heavens. Allow it to help you stand a little taller.
- *Envision yourself surrounded by a beautiful, protective circle of light.* Gold is a wonderful protective color, but go with whatever feels right or comes up naturally.
- *State aloud or in your mind, "I am protected. Only that which is for my highest good may enter this space."* If this phrase doesn't work for you, experiment until you find the words that feel most powerful to you.

What happens from here depends on your comfort level. If you want to communicate with the spirit, state your boundaries before proceeding. For instance, you may tell the spirit, "I'm willing to talk to you and listen to what you want, but you have to leave when I say so." See what kind of a response you get back. If the spirit seems agreeable, move forward with the remaining steps. However, if the vibe feels off or hostile or you experience something threatening, it's time to claim your space. State loudly and firmly, "My name is [state your name] and I claim this space as mine. All spirits and entities must leave this space *immediately*." Repeat four times. Imagine yourself getting larger each time you say it. I suggest leaving your circle of protection in place until you know the spirit has departed. Wait until you feel safe before releasing and cleansing.

MAKE IT YOUR OWN

I hope the steps provided here bring you closer to the spiritual world. They have been developed through a lot of practice over time. That said, give yourself the freedom to experiment and make this practice fit your unique style, needs, and abilities.

Please journal on the following:

+ What worked well for you?
+ What needs to be adapted?
+ What is something new that you could incorporate into your practice?

CHAPTER 8
BELLS AND WHISTLES

While it is important to practice mediumship without the use of tools so you don't become dependent on them, there are so many fun props that can bolster and reinforce your own natural abilities. The following outlines some of the "bells and whistles" you can incorporate into your practice. Remember that at the end of the day, these are just things. You are what makes them magical. Speak to your tools and remind them of their purpose. The more you do this and the more you practice, the better they will work for you.

CLASSIC DIVINATION TOOLS

The following describes some of the most common tools used in mediumship and other forms of divination.

Water—It bears repeating that water is magical. A glass of water can serve as refreshment for spirits who have made the journey back to the realm of the living. A bowl of water can serve as a conduit for spirits, enhancing the communication between our worlds. In some traditions, a dish of water is placed alongside a bar of soap, towel, and mirror on ancestor altars, particularly during times when the veil between worlds is especially thin, such as Día de los Muertos and Samhain. Whisper thanks to the water and ask for its assistance in communicating with the dead. When the water has served its purpose, use it to water plants either in your house or outside. Water is becoming more precious as our climate changes and extreme weather and drought become the norm. Treating water with reverence in our spiritual practice will also remind us to value it in our everyday lives.

Candles—Candles don't just provide ambiance during spirit communication. They serve as a beacon so spirits can find their way. The element of fire provides an energy boost that spirits can use as they communicate. You can charge your candles by holding them in your hands and focusing your mind on what you want them to do. You can add extra magic by anointing them in an appropriate divination oil. You can follow this by rolling them in dried, crushed plants that you have "woken up" by asking them to assist you in connecting with the spirit world. Some suggested plants and tips for making simple divination oils are included in the "around the house" folk magic recipes at the end of this chapter.

Incense—Smoke can provide a powerful boost to our communication with spirits. Smoke is said to carry our prayers to other realms. The smoke represents the element of air, which correlates with communication. Incense can also serve as "food" for spirits when blended with appropriate plants and resins. For example, coffee and tobacco can be used in incense as a treat for spirits. Grind them into a fine powder with a mortar and pestle and burn them on a charcoal disk in a heatproof container.

Pendulums—A pendulum is a weight that is suspended from a string or chain. Many of them are made from carved crystals, but you can use necklaces, keys, or anything else that can be dangled from a chain or string. Pendulums are usually held in the hand, which offers a fixed point that allows the pendulum to swing with ease. When talking with spirits, you can ask them to move the pendulum to answer your questions. Pendulums are often used in yes-no-maybe questions, so you must establish which direction indicates each answer. For example, right for yes, left for no, side to side for maybe. The most common criticism of pendulums is that our unconscious fine motor skills, also referred to as ideomotor responses, are responsible for their movement. On the flip side, it is also possible that spirits are able to harness our energy to move the pendulum with ease. You can eliminate the ideomotor response by using a pendulum stand, which is a fixed object that your pendulum can hang from. You will get less movement, but the results are interesting when they occur.

Pen and paper—Humble paper and pen become a fascinating spirit communication tool when you use them for automatic writing. When talking to spirits, allow your mind to become gentle. You may even enter a light trance state if you feel comfortable doing so. You can ask the spirit to speak through your hand onto the paper. Let your hand squiggle across the paper, writing or drawing unconsciously. Don't try to read it or make sense of it as your hand is moving. Some people find that using their nondominant hand yields better results. Look for words or pictures that provide answers to your questions.

Spirit boards—Also called talking boards or Ouija boards, which is a brand name, spirit boards are perhaps the best-known spirit communication tool out there. They are a board containing the twenty-six letters of the alphabet, numbers zero through nine, and the words *yes*, *no*, and *goodbye*. Spirit boards are most commonly used in séances and have quite a role in many horror movies. The theory is that the energy of the group assists spirits to communicate by spelling out their answers. Members of the séance gently rest their fingertips on either a planchette, which is a flat, heart-shaped pointer, or an overturned glass. The planchette or glass will move as the spirit responds to questions. This is another example of ideomotor actions coming into play. As with pendulums, the criticism of spirit boards is that the group's unconscious actions are what drives the planchette's movements. The counterargument is that spirits can harness the group's energy and their unconscious motor skills to move the planchette. While I don't consider spirit boards to be intrinsically good or bad, they need to be used with care. When conducting a spirit board session, everyone should ensure they are grounded and protected and that the mediumship session is closed properly. If these steps are taken, you should have nothing to worry about.

Divination—Classic divination practices include reading tarot, oracle, or playing cards; throwing bones; and reading tea leaves, to name just a few. You can incorporate your divination practices into mediumship by simply asking the spirits to speak to you through your divination tools.

Scrying—Scrying is a type of divination that warrants its own discussion. Scrying is the process of staring into a reflective surface while focusing on what you wish to see or the question you want answered. You can also scry with fire by staring into the flame of a candle or fire. Mirrors, particularly black mirrors, and bowls of water are two of the most common scrying mediums. You can make a black scrying mirror by painting the backside of the glass of a picture frame and adding a piece of black velvet behind it for additional depth. You will most likely see images in your mind rather than clearly reflected in the surface of your mirror or water. Scrying oils can also add to your practice. To enhance your communication with spirits of the dead, mix a carrier oil such as olive oil or fractionated coconut oil with dried marigold flowers in a small bottle. Marigolds have a long connection with spirits of the dead. Do something to "wake up" the spirits of the flowers prior to adding them. Speak to them, ask for their help, and gently blow on them, waking them up with your breath. Focus your intention on your scrying oil every time you use it. Perhaps even come up with a brief mantra you say each time you use the oil. You can anoint your scrying mirror with your oil before each use. I personally always ask my scrying mirror, which is one of my favorite tools, to "help me see what is unseen, and hear what is unsaid." If you are using water as your scrying medium, you can pour some oil into the bowl and look for images as the oil swirls around.

Dowsing rods—Dowsing rods are one of the few divination tools to have some public legitimacy, particularly for things like finding sources of underground water or precious metals. Dowsing is practiced by holding two rods or sticks, often made from copper or certain types of wood, like hazel or willow. The dowser, which is the person holding the rods, holds their arms at a 90 degree angle and asks their question. It is an affirmative answer when the rods cross, forming an X. For example, if a person is looking for water, they would dig where the dowsing rods cross. Dowsing rods are helpful mediumship tools that work very similarly to pendulums. They work well with yes-no questions and can also point if you are looking for something specific. This is helpful when looking for spirits in haunted spaces. I will ask where the spirits are located and follow the direction the rods point. When they cross, I know I have found the right location. Once again, the ideomotor response is frequently cited as the reason for the dowsing rod movements. That said, if it works, it works.

Crystals—The energy of the earth itself can be found in crystals. Many people use crystals and rocks in their spiritual practice because they are easy to use. You can benefit from their energy by simply carrying them in your pocket, wearing them as jewelry, or placing them on your altars. Here are some of my favorite crystals for mediumship.

+ *Citrine*—If you want a negativity buster that doesn't need to be cleansed, amber-colored citrine is for you. Keep a citrine crystal under your pillow to ward off spirits wanting to disturb your slumber or in your pocket as you explore haunted locations.

+ *Black tourmaline*—Inky black tourmaline soaks up dark energy like a sponge. It is protective, grounding, and excellent for those struggling with fear-based emotions to have on hand during mediumship sessions.

+ *Labradorite*—Associated with the darker and more mysterious aspects of the moon, labradorite always makes me think of the High Priestess in the tarot. Labradorite can be used to enhance spiritual and magical abilities and offer protection to those who access dark and liminal spaces. You may find a labradorite palm stone or pendant brings you additional confidence in your abilities as a medium.

+ *Aura quartz*—The iridescent rainbow shimmer of aura quartz can raise your vibration and simply cheer you up. These crystals are made when quartz is heated and fused with the vapors of precious metals like silver, gold, and platinum. While their beauty is not naturally occurring, they are an incredible example of alchemy. They are a perfect stone to raise your vibration after a mediumship session.

+ *Celestine*—Baby-blue celestine carries sweet, peaceful energy and is known to assist in connecting with angels. Hold a piece of celestine when invoking the archangels in your grounding practice prior to mediumship.

+ *Dirt and rocks*—Dirt and rocks that are thoughtfully collected from meaningful locations can be powerfully attractive to spirits. Rocks from the hometown of a spirit you want to talk to or dirt from near the front door of their beloved home can be placed with your spirit offerings prior to a mediumship session. Take only small amounts and always leave a respectful, litter-free offering, such as a pour of water, in return.

PARANORMAL INVESTIGATION TOOLS

The following describes some of the paranormal investigation tools that can make mediumship extra fun. Any of these tools can be incorporated into your solo conversations with spirits, group séances, or explorations of haunted locations. I have chosen to limit this list to the tools I have experience using, but there is a wide world of ever-evolving devices available from the paranormal field.

EMF meter—Devices designed to measure electromagnetic fields. They are used to detect the levels of and changes in electric or magnetic energy in an area. Some people believe that spirits emit an electromagnetic charge that can be detected using these devises. Having an EMF meter as you explore haunted locations or close by as you conduct a mediumship session can help you identify when you are in the presence of spirits.

REM Pod—A type of EMF detector that radiates an electromagnetic field from its antenna. It has a small, round base with an antenna rising from the top along with several lights. When something breaks the field, a light and buzzer go off. It also has a temperature gauge that indicates increases and decreases in temperature. It can be triggered erroneously by cell phones and other electronic objects as well as open windows, candles, and anything else that affects temperature. Regardless, this is one of my favorite tools to use in my mediumship because it often provides external validation for what I experience through my clair senses.

Spirit box—Spirit boxes, also referred to as ghost boxes, are AM/FM radios that are modified to quickly scan through radio frequencies, creating a white noise effect. The theory is that spirits are able to utilize that white noise and manipulate it to form words and phrases. The criticism, of course, is that our minds latch onto snippets of words on the radio, filling in the blanks to hear what we want to hear. However, too many people have had powerful experiences using these devices to discount them completely. All spirit boxes are modeled after something called the Frank's Box, which was created by a man named Frank Sumption. Mr. Sumption created his first ghost box device in 2002, claiming he received the instructions from the spirit world. He only made one hundred eighty of them, and he gave them to people, free of charge, whom he and the spirits saw fit.

Recorder—The voice memo app on our smartphones is one of the most easily accessible spirit communication devices we have. They are a way of capturing something called EVP evidence, which stands for electronic voice phenomena. Simply press record, sit quietly, and ask questions, leaving plenty of time for spirits to answer. Then play it back to see if you caught anything. The great thing about cell phone apps is that you can see the soundwaves, which may help you identify any anomalies. It is helpful to keep your EVP sessions short and listen to them immediately after so you don't miss messages that may warrant follow-up questions. Staying still is also important because the smallest rustle—as well as growling stomachs—can trick you. The voices captured don't usually sound like normal human ones. They often sound like whispers or grunts and can be difficult to decipher.

Video cameras—Setting up a video camera during your mediumship sessions and séances or while you explore haunted locations can sometimes identify strange occurrences you wouldn't have noticed otherwise. There are many low-cost cameras that link to our smartphones, including some that are motion activated, or you can use the camera on your phone. I regularly use a spirit box and I always try to get video of my sessions. I find that there are often words or sentences I miss in the moment. If you are in a group, ensure all parties agree to be recorded and do not share footage publicly without everyone's consent.

Experimentation

While I love a good gadget, everyday items and a little creativity can be turned into interesting paranormal experiments. The sky is truly the limit here. Here are a couple of suggestions to get you thinking:

- Set out two movement-activated toys or lights. Either label them "yes" and "no" or have two distinct colors. Ask spirits to answer simple questions by setting off the devices.
- Lightweight balls and balloons can be placed around the room of your séance or mediumship session. Tell spirits they are welcome to play with them or move them to let you know they are present. Use common sense and eliminate all possibility they could be moved by a draft.
- Property records and historical information. When we have paranormal experiences, it can be hard to shake the desire to know more about who we encountered and why they are there. While many records require in-person visits to government offices, there is a lot of information available online. Home listings through realty websites, historical society websites, online property records, and creative browser search terms can lead you to interesting information.

That concludes our brief overview of paranormal investigation tools. It has barely scratched the surface of what exists. I hope it inspires you to have fun and get creative.

"AROUND THE HOUSE" FOLK MAGIC
RECIPES TO ENHANCE YOUR PRACTICE

Now that we have covered classic divination tools as well as the ones where batteries are required, let's close out with some folk magic. The following provides two divination oil recipes and one for a salt scrub or bath. Divination oils are a way to reinforce your inner work and intention setting.[25] You can rub a small amount on your feet, third eye, neck, belly button, and/or pulse points. You can also use the oils to anoint candles or your divination tools.

A variety of herbs are listed in the following recipes.[26] Choose the ones you feel connected to. Talk to them and ask them to help with what you'd like to do. Listen to any messages you receive. If they don't want to serve that purpose, use a different herb. If they agree, thank them. All the herbs described below tend to play nicely with others. You can mix and match the herbs from the different recipes if that feels right.

For either recipe, start by pouring two or three shot glass-size amounts of a carrier oil such as fractionated coconut oil, jojoba oil, or even olive oil into a small jar.

I encourage you to get creative and think about how you can activate the oils for their intended purpose. You can create a prayer that you speak over the oil prior to each use. You can make them during a full moon or during an auspicious astrological time. You can even bury the jar in a meaningful location and dig it up after a predetermined number of days. As I have said before, the more you charge your tools, the better they will work for you.

---

25. While it is good practice to make your own materials, I highly recommend the divination oils made by the Death Witch, run by Loretta Ledesma, as well as the spiritual oils made by Madame Pamita's Parlour of Wonders. They are literally bottled magic.

26. One of my favorite "quick-guide" resources for magical herbs is *Materia Magica* by Draja Mickaharic. Details are included in the Recommended Reading list.

Psychic Awareness Oil

Use before spirit communication sessions to increase your psychic awareness. Add one to three pinches of the following herbs to your carrier oil.

- Orris root—A plant of many names. Also called Queen Elizabeth root, orris root is the humble iris bulb. It improves communication between people and the physical and astral worlds. This is a great use for irises that need to be separated. Just chop the root and dry in the oven on low heat.
- Celery seed—Supports astral communication and combines well with orris root.
- Chamomile—Strengthens the connection of astral and mental bodies. Brings calm fortitude to your work.
- Calendula or marigold—Brings the astral realm closer. Has a close connection with spirits of the dead.

Vibration Raising Oil

Use this oil after cleansing to lift your vibration.

Add one to three pinches of the following herbs to your carrier oil.

- Basil—Offers protection. Lightens energy and brings a positive influence.
- Rosemary—Raises vibration. Enhances memory and clear thinking.
- Fenugreek—Clears the mind and removes influences of others.
- Angelica root—Also referred to as the Root of the Holy Ghost, angelica root has a strong connection to Archangel Michael. Used for protection from danger and illness.

Purifying Salt Scrub or Bath

For cleansing after spirit contact.

+ Carrier oil, if preparing as a scrub.

+ Salt—Acts as a purifier.

+ Rue—Effective in combating malintent and the evil eye.

+ Eucalyptus—Associated with the element of air, eucalyptus promotes clear thinking and purification. Brings a breath of fresh air.

+ Hyssop—A biblical plant used in the ceremonial cleaning of people and their homes. Purifies the body and spirit.

For a cleansing bath, mix one cup of salt and a small pinch of one to three of the suggested herb options. Pour at least half the mixture into your bath and fully immerse yourself no less than three times. For a salt scrub, mix one cup of salt, one to three of the suggested herb options, and enough carrier oil to make a paste. Use in the shower or on your hands and feet to cleanse away residual energy from spirits you have come in contact with. Regardless of which technique you use, drip dry and dress in clean clothes.

CHAPTER 9
HAUNTED PLACES, PEOPLE, AND THINGS

This chapter will provide an overview of the types of hauntings that can afflict people, places, and things, along with basic steps you can take to address hauntings on your own. I have found that almost everyone has a story or two of unexplained phenomena in a physical location. However, hauntings are not necessarily confined to homes or physical structures. There are haunted forests, like the famed Hoia-Baciu Forest in Romania; haunted parks, like Cheeseman Park in Denver, Colorado; and haunted roads, like Riverdale Road in Thornton, Colorado. Objects can also be haunted, which means that wherever they are, spirit activity is sure to follow. Many of us have heard of certain famous haunted dolls, but any type of object can have spiritual attachments. People can also find themselves with spirits anchored to them, which means they are the epicenter of any paranormal activity.

Yet another complicating factor is that there are different types of hauntings and, as we discussed in earlier chapters, different types of spirits that will require different kinds of intervention. Every situation is—you guessed it—different. It can be a difficult and time-consuming process to suss out the core of a haunting, but it is a worthwhile endeavor if you want to better understand what is happening. This is especially true if you hope to make things better for the living humans experiencing the activity, which can in many cases also improve circumstances for the spirits themselves.

There is a limit to what one can learn to do safely from a book. Situations that require higher levels of intervention should be handled by an experienced spiritual professional. I provide tips on how to find trustworthy spiritual and magical workers as well as red flags for spotting fraud in the final chapter of this book.

SIGNS YOU HAVE A HAUNTED SPACE ON YOUR HANDS

When people contact me about unexplained activity, usually in their homes or another physical location, I ask for information on the following three categories:

+ *Physical disturbances* such as, but not limited to, knockings, footsteps, items moving, or electrical issues that can't be explained.
+ *Mental disturbances* such as disturbing dreams, mood changes, confusion, or intrusive thoughts that don't feel like one's own.
+ *Visual occurrences* such as seeing figures, mist, or shadows.

Prior to agreeing to help with a haunting, I ask that people first look for electrical, plumbing, and structural problems; assess the health of everyone who is making these reports; and generally take the time to make sure what they are experiencing can't be explained by something rational. While this may sound like a buzzkill, I promise that it's worth your time. What initially seems like strange and supernatural activity can often be linked to something completely mundane. Let me share one of my more embarrassing stories to illustrate this point.

I once worked on the fifth floor of a commercial office building in East Denver. It's not the type of place you would think of as haunted. One day, my coworkers and I began swapping stories about strange happenings in our office. Many of us had seen a man in our suite and heard voices and knocking when no one was around. In the morning, we would come in to find every office door closed.

We assumed it was the cleaning staff that came at night, but they claimed that wasn't something they did. Lights would sometimes turn on, seemingly by themselves, and doors would swing shut on their own. I asked a woman who worked down the hall if anything unexplained ever happened in her space. She rolled her eyes and nodded. She said she would often walk past one particular office and see a man sitting at the desk. She'd do a double take and he'd vanish.

According to someone familiar with the building's history, it sat on the grounds of a former Catholic girls' orphanage that burned to the ground in the 1960s. Supposedly some of the girls had died in the fire. Another person had leaped to their death from the roof of the neighboring building in the 1990s, and people on the top floor often heard voices coming through the vents. We learned that most of the cleaning and maintenance workers had also experienced many of the same things we had—voices, doors opening and closing, lights turning on, and flashes of people who would vanish upon a second glance. After learning all this, I went on high alert for evidence of paranormal activity around the office.

One Friday, I stayed late. There was an evening event at my son's school, and I had some time to fill before heading over. I made a casserole that needed to be reheated, so I popped it into the toaster oven in our kitchen and went back to my office. I got lost in whatever I was doing, and my concentration was broken by a loud "DING!" I rushed to the kitchen and found that the toaster oven had turned off, seemingly by itself, and my casserole was perfectly browned. In fact, if it had cooked for much longer, it would have burned. I couldn't figure out how this had happened. I had no memory of turning on the timer and had intended to just watch the clock. Did our office spirit take pity on me and save my casserole? That had to be the most logical explanation.

I went to my son's event and couldn't wait to tell my husband about this new experience when I got home. I told my mom when we talked that Sunday and was so excited to tell my coworkers. On Monday, I told my new story with true gusto, having practiced it a few times by this point. Once I was done, my boss said quietly, "Sterling, you can't turn on the toaster without turning on the timer."

She was right.

This moment defined my commitment to healthy skepticism. We can easily trick ourselves into thinking that something is unexplained or paranormal when it's really a byproduct of an active imagination or coincidence. A healthy way to approach any suspected spirit encounter is to first take stock of the most banal possible explanations. Let's say you took photographs in a supposedly haunted location and your pictures have orbs in them. These glowing circles can indicate spirit activity and you can sometimes even see faces or other images in them if you zoom in. Before you declare victory in capturing evidence of life after death, ask yourself a few questions. Is the lens on your camera dirty? Was the location dusty? Are the orbs in the same spot on every picture? Take a few more shots somewhere with similar lighting and see if you get the same thing. You may find that, disappointing as it may be, you had a few spots on your camera lens and there is nothing to get excited about.

This doesn't always have to end in disappointment. When we take the time to assess mundane causes of strange activity, we may still determine that there is something paranormal at play. For example, in 2019, I was in Washington, DC for work and stayed in a wonderful hotel that was built in the 1930s and rich with history. On the first night of my stay, the motion sensor light in my closet kept coming on when I was nowhere near it. It was accompanied by an uncomfortable feeling of being watched and started to scare the heck out of me. After the first few times it happened, I took some deep, slow breaths to calm down and dragged a chair into the closet so I could inspect the light. There weren't any bugs that could have set it off and I couldn't identify anything else that could affect the sensor. There was construction on some of the lower floors and it was an old building. There could have been electrical issues, but that was impossible for me to determine. I was in that room for four nights, and by the end of the third night, I was confident that a spirit was teasing me. I ended up telling whoever it was to "knock it off, please," and kept the closet door shut so it wasn't quite as creepy. Can I prove this was actually caused by a spirit? Nope. At the end of the day, I can't prove any of these stories, but that doesn't mean they aren't real and true.

My last suggestion for embracing healthy skepticism is to use historical research when you can. Libraries often have access to historical property records. Many city records are public, and even your local police department can run a search on calls to an address. Some records, particularly police reports, do require a fee to access. If you can validate experiences you are having with factual information, it will help you better diagnose what is happening.

Even once you have worked to debunk your own experiences, many of you will find you still have unexplained phenomena on your hands. In my experience, there are two types of hauntings.

PLACES THAT MAINTAIN
VIBRATIONS OF POWERFUL EVENTS

Sometimes when I tap into the energy of a location, it doesn't feel like something that is playing out in real time. It's more like a reel of film, or a story that is on repeat with no connection to current reality. These events range from the tragic, like a loop of a murder or suicide, to the mundane, like a whisper of someone's past morning routine of having coffee and reading the paper. These types of hauntings are like an energetic transfer print that is left on a physical location. Hauntings caused by conjured spirits may have similarities to residual hauntings because they were created, either intentionally or unintentionally, by the dedicated or repeated action or intention of others, rather than a being with independent, intelligent consciousness.

SENTIENT SPIRIT ACTIVITY

This is what most of us think of when we talk about haunted houses. These are spirits who can engage with the living intelligently. Some spirits can instigate poltergeist activity by making noise, moving objects, or otherwise creating change in their environment. This is particularly noticeable for people who aren't tuned in to the more subtle types of communication. As we discussed earlier, physical manifestations can also be signs of elemental spirits.

WHAT'S HAUNTED? PEOPLE, PLACES, OR THINGS?

When experiencing paranormal activity, we need to assess to the best of our ability what is the heart of the haunting.

Spirit Attachments to People

When activity only happens when a certain person is in the home and the activity seems to follow them when they leave, that likely means the individual has a spirit attached to them. When I bring up the concept of spirit attachments, the first thing most people think of is possession. A far more common occurrence is for wayward spirits to become stuck to a person. Sometimes this is because the living person reminds the spirit of someone they knew in life or they develop some form of concern for the living person. Bad-tempered spirits who enjoy scaring people may attach in order to feed off people's fear. There are also lost souls that are simply drawn to the light of a living person and latch on out of confusion. As we discussed previously, practicing discernment techniques that allow you to notice where your thoughts, feelings, and energy end and where the influence of an external spirit begins is crucial for identifying spirit attachments. Remember that you have the upper hand over any spirits simply by being alive. When you are being bothered by a spirit, come back to the meditations in this book to help you ground and protect your energy. As we touched on in the chapter on negative entities, if someone experiences what they believe is a spirit that is causing or encouraging them to hurt themselves or someone else, they must seek a mental and physical health evaluation before pursuing magical or spiritual assistance.

Remedies for Spirit Attachment

The following tips are some old-timey remedies to help those with spirit attachments get some rest and relief.

Camphor

Camphor is a powerful spirit repellant and magical purifier. It is one of my favorite ingredients to use with meddlesome spirits. You can purchase camphor crystals at many botanicas and metaphysical shops and it can be used in a variety of ways.

It can be burned as incense on a charcoal disk in a heatproof container. Waft the smoke over yourself and the space in need of clearing while visualizing the smoke pushing out all unwanted spirits. Make sure your windows are open so the spirits can leave.

You can place a spoonful of camphor in a glass of water and set it on your bedside table or underneath your bed. Discard the water in the morning, either flushing it down the toilet or pouring it out in the sink, and refresh it each night. You can do this until you are ready to try sleeping without it. This is particularly helpful for reducing nightmares caused by spirit attachments.

Camphor is also a key ingredient in a common household item with a powerful magical history: vapor rubs. Years ago, I had the opportunity to ask an experienced conjure worker what he would recommend when I was dealing with a disruptive spirit that had followed me home after exploring a haunted location. He smirked and said that all I needed was a jar of Vicks VapoRub. I smirked back, thinking he was pulling my leg. He patiently explained how vapor rubs are a remedy for many ailments, but that in the case of pestering spirits, the camphor, menthol, and eucalyptus are strong magical purifiers. It is also amplified by its one-hundred-plus-year history of people using it as a magical cure. These days you can even find lovely small batch versions made with natural ingredients.

If you are experiencing spirit attachments that are disrupting your life, you can use vapor rub on your feet, belly button, temples, and neck. If you experience tension in other places on your body, use vapor rub on those areas as well. Do this twice a day, stating out loud that the spirit attached to you must leave your space and that they are not welcome. Do this until you experience a shift.

If spirits bother you while you sleep, you can use vapor rub on the headboard and footboard of your bed.

Salt

Salt is widely known as another magical purifier. It is also a handy spirit repellent. To annoy and repel a spirit that is attached to you, make a simple salt scrub. You can use the recipe from chapter 8 or mix any salt you have handy and cooking oil, such as olive oil. As you blend your salt scrub into the consistency of mud, state your intention that as the scrub is applied to your body, all spirits attached to you must leave immediately. Use the scrub in the shower a couple of times per week, stating your intention as you do so. After getting out of the shower, envision yourself flooded with bright light and held in a circle of protection.

You have the right to be safe in your own body. I have found that most spirits will move on once they understand they are not welcome. If they don't, that is your cue to seek out a skilled practitioner who can assist you.

Spiritual Attachments to Things

Spirits can attach to objects in the same way they can attach to people and physical locations. That means that anywhere these objects are, paranormal activity is sure to follow. When attempting to identify the heart of a haunting, it can be tricky to pinpoint when an object is the culprit. For example, in my home, we have a bedroom mirror with some form of spirit attachment. It belonged to one of my husband's grandmothers and is over one hundred years old. Unexplained noises, nightmares, and feelings of being watched were common in that bedroom, but we never attributed the mirror as the cause until one family member said they saw a male figure appear in the mirror on more than one occasion.

We started paying more attention to the mirror and discovered that it appears to be the epicenter of what occurs in that room. Traditional mediumship efforts to connect with any spirits attached to the mirror weren't very successful, and I often found myself confused after trying. I began using my investigation tools, specifically my REM Pod, dowsing rods, and spirit box, to better understand what was happening. I had the most success with my REM Pod, which has a temperature gauge and radiates an electromagnetic field that beeps when it is broken. When I spoke directly to any spirits attached to the mirror, something appeared to break the electromagnetic field around the device, and the temperature seemed to fluctuate when this happened. The mirror was close to a window, but even in summer months with the air-conditioning turned off and the window closed, the area close to the mirror was noticeably colder than the rest of the room. I was able to have what felt like intelligent conversations with whatever was attached to the mirror, asking questions and requesting that any spirits make the REM Pod beep in response. It didn't happen every time, but often enough that it seemed meaningful. Requests to any spirits in the mirror to respect the space of the person staying there were not productive, so for a time, I focused on cleansing and spirit repelling techniques. I would wash the mirror with Florida water. I would then apply vapor rub to the mirror, declaring that any portal attached to it was closed. This was somewhat successful. We would receive periods of quiet, but the activity would generally resume.

What to Do with Haunted Objects

We have three options when it comes to haunted objects:

1. Learn to live with it.
2. Get rid of the item.
3. Attempt to remove the spirit.

The first two options are self-explanatory. If you decide to part with the object, be honest about the item's history. It is both the right thing to do and, for some people, a selling point. There's a market for haunted objects and the internet makes it easy to connect with people who want what you wish to be rid of.

The third option is much trickier, and your plan of action will need to be guided by the type of attachment. The following are three common attachment types.

Residual Attachment

Residual attachments are like a memory imprinted on an object. This seems to cause others to witness the activity or experience the emotions linked to the original source. For example, if an object in your home causes you to feel strong emotions that don't feel like your own, it could be due to imprinted, residual energy that was left behind by a previous owner.

PSYCHOMETRY PRACTICE FOR ASSESSING RESIDUAL ATTACHMENTS

Psychometry is the art of receiving psychic and mediumistic impressions from objects. You can use this practice to cultivate your discernment of residual energy that has been left on objects. This involves a field trip, so bring your mediumship grimoire with you and record your experiences.

Visit an antique store. Take a few moments to get to neutral and ground before going in. You may find it helpful to assess your baseline, like you did in the meditation for identifying your clair senses.

Focus on one item you feel drawn to. Observe how you feel when you handle the item. Do your emotions change? Do you experience thoughts that don't feel like your own? Do you see anything in your mind? If you experience any of these, you may have encountered an item with residual spirit attachments. Compare what you experienced with your baseline and document it in your grimoire.

Release your connection to the item. Do a quick cleansing visualization before you move on.

Conjured Spirits or Thoughtforms

As we discussed in chapter 5, spirit activity can be created by dedicated or repetitive actions, and some magical traditions involve conjuring spirits for both malevolent and benevolent purposes. Once manifested, the spirits can be anchored to physical objects. Do not try this at home, kids. This type of magical work is not to be approached cavalierly.

Thoughtforms can also be created in more mundane ways. Let's say a child has a favorite stuffed animal that has been their best friend since they were a baby. They give it a very formed personality, and to them, their "stuffie" becomes a living, breathing companion. If the child also has natural psychic or magical gifts, this experience may be amplified. As the child grows up, they may leave their old pal behind. Perhaps the doll becomes the plaything of a new child, who somehow perceives the same personality of this new-to-them object. This is a benign example, but it hopefully illustrates the way objects can hold energy.

Sentient Spirits Using an Object as a Vessel
I tend to think of this situation in the same way I approach spaces that are haunted by intelligent spirits. This is explored at length toward the end of this chapter, but unless the activity is malicious or aggressive, I advise one start by approaching the situation with kindness, calmness, and establishment of boundaries.

Living with Haunted Objects
If you choose to keep the object, you can attempt to neutralize its energy by regularly wiping it down with Florida water or salt water or cleansing the object with camphor smoke. As you do so, focus all your energy on your goal. If the object is small, you can place it in a box resting on a bed of salt with some citrine crystals tucked around it. Be mindful about where you keep haunted objects. Place them away from the heart of your home and do not keep them where people sleep.

I find that haunted objects and haunted places can be managed in a similar fashion. Because there are so many parallels, feel free to adapt any of the haunted place suggestions for use with haunted objects.

Haunted Places

If spirit activity seems to be connected solely to a physical location, the first option you always have is to try to ignore it. This works decently with imprinted energy and residual hauntings because, as we discussed earlier, they are like movie clips on repeat. Strong residual hauntings may present like intelligent spirits, but over time it will become apparent that the activity is repetitive and does not seem to be affected by attempts to interact. While residual hauntings can be caused by traumatic events, they can also be caused by mundane activities, such as someone who smoked on their back porch with their morning coffee for decades. People may report hearing the strike of a match or they may continue to smell tobacco or coffee around the same time of day.

If the activity is consistent and doesn't seem to change based on the actions of the living, it is likely you are experiencing a residual haunting that may dissipate with regular, intentional cleansing.

Basic Cleansing for Residual Hauntings

A few cleansing suggestions are provided below. While this section is specific to residual hauntings, these suggestions can be used anytime you need to cleanse and reset the energy in your space.

New Brooms and the Magic of Sweeping

A fabulous old-timey way of clearing out stagnant energy in a home with noncarpeted floors is to get a new broom and do an intentional energetic sweep. Some practitioners I know will even get a new broom at the start of the new year. I am someone who likes to use household tools until they fall apart. If you are like me, or if getting a new broom will be challenging for you, thoroughly wash the bristles of your current broom on a regular basis and each time prior to conducting an energetic deep cleaning of your space.

Sweep your home from top floor to bottom floor, back to front, while focusing on clearing out old, unhelpful energy along with the dust and dirt. If possible, sweep straight out the front door. Keep your windows open while you sweep if you can. For very stubborn energy, you can do a second sweep of your home using salt as an additional purifier. Sprinkle salt on your floors while focusing on the intention of purifying your space, then once again sweep your home from top to bottom, back to front.

Here is another option from my personal practice. I have a besom, which is a traditional handmade broom, that hangs on my wall and is only used for energetic sweeping. It never touches the floor. When I need to clear out the energy of my home, I will "sweep" the air close to the floor with my besom.

Floor Washes

Floor washes are one of my favorite ways to energetically clean. They are used in many magical traditions, and I have developed my own recipes and techniques over the years.

When I need to assertively clear out stagnant or negative energy, my go-to floor wash is a bucket of hot water with a half cup of white vinegar, nine drops of lemon essential oil, and a fat pinch of salt. As I mix the ingredients, I state the intention that this blend will remove negativity from my home. Some may find this controversial as vinegar and lemon are used as cursing agents in some traditions, but I have found that this blend is very effective.

If you are working to clear out a very persistent residual haunting, it may be helpful to follow up with a second floor wash that is focused on what you want to cultivate in your home. As we've discussed, a common mistake many of us make in cleansing work is that we neglect to fill a cleansed space with something desirable, such as blessings, love, and a sense of abundance. I love floor washes because we can customize them based on what we need. I encourage you to learn about the folklore and traditional uses and personalities of plants, particularly those that are native to where you live and connected to your own cultures of origin.

Here is a simple floor wash recipe with easy-to-find herbs that strikes a balance of calling in protection, abundance, love, and joy. Fill a large pot with clean, cold water. Take a moment to be grateful for the gift of clean running water and ask the water to serve as a carrier for the work you are about to do. As you bring your pot of water to a boil, gather the following:

- 9 whole cloves for protection
- 1 tablespoon of rose petals for love
- 1 tablespoon of lavender for peace
- 1 cinnamon stick for abundance and blessings
- 1 tablespoon of orange peel for friendship

Before you add each ingredient, ask it to serve the purposes listed above. Gently breathe on the ingredients to fully wake them up. Remember that magical and energetic work require more than just throwing materials together. The more you wake up and work your ingredients, the stronger their effect will be.

After you speak your intention to each herb, add it to the pot. Allow it to simmer until it has the appearance of a strong tea. Add one cup of floor wash to one gallon of water and mop your home from top to bottom, back to front. You can also use this blend to wipe down commonly used surfaces such as light switches and door-knobs or for cleansing objects with residual attachments. Keep any leftovers in the fridge for up to one week. Discard any excess outside.

Smoke Cleansing

If you live in a space with lots of carpet, sweeping and floor washes will only get you so far. Smoke cleansing is another wonderful way to cleanse your space. It's also a good option for cleansing haunted objects. Please do not use white sage, palo santo, or copal to cleanse your home unless it is part of your own cultural heritage. These are culturally specific medicines that are endangered and overharvested. Develop relationships with cleansing plants that are either native to your area or linked to your own cultural heritage. It's an additional bonus if you can grow or responsibly forage them yourself.

Many metaphysical shops make their own incense blends for clearing, cleansing, and more. You can also use herbal smoke wands or tree resins. I live in the Western United States where pine trees grow abundantly. A couple of times per year, I will collect small amounts of pine resin. I take only a small amount from each tree and only after I ask the tree for and wait until I am granted permission. We can and should listen to the natural world the same way we listen to spirits. I leave an offering of water, a precious resource in the West, in exchange. I use the pine resin as an incense, which I burn on a charcoal disk in a heatproof container to cleanse and bless my home. When I visit my family in Wyoming, I will forage native arte-misia, which is a type of sage, in the same manner I collect pine resin. I tend to do this once per year over Midsommar, which is an import-ant holiday in the trolldom tradition. I dry and use the artemisia to make my own smoke wands with additional herbs and flowers that I grow in my garden, such as lavender and mugwort. I use the smoke wands to cleanse and cultivate positive energy. Take the time to connect with the materials you use, and you will be rewarded with a clear and peaceful home.

Hauntings by Sentient Spirits

When experiencing paranormal activity caused by what appears to be sentient, intelligent spirits, the first reaction most people have is to do whatever they can to get rid of the cause of the disturbances. This is not what I advise people to start with, but I understand the reasons why people feel the way they do. Hauntings can be very traumatizing for some people. It sucks to feel scared of something you can't fully understand or see and that may not communicate clearly. However, in my experience, many hauntings are caused by spirits who want to be seen and are frustrated by being stuck in between. If the first thing you try is evicting a spirit that has likely been in a physical location far longer than you have, they may leave or go dormant temporarily, but then they may come back more aggressively. Spirits don't exactly care about tenant rights.

While I understand why the first response folks have is to show spirits the door, diplomacy can yield much better results. I suggest people first approach their resident spirits with an attitude of "sit down and join me for a cup of tea and a conversation." If that doesn't work, then it's a different story.

Start with Cleansing, a Conversation, and Ground Rules

Start with clearing your home and yourself using some of the techniques described earlier in this chapter. They will help dissipate negativity and raise your vibration, which may make communication a bit easier.

Instigate a cordial conversation with your household spirits in the location where the activity is centered. If the activity is all over the place, start in what feels like the heart of the space. Set out a glass of water, a candle, and a small food offering. Go through the spirit communication steps 1 through 3.

When you are calm, grounded, and protected, light your candle and say out loud that you would like to speak with the spirits in the space that have been interacting with you. Even though this is no one's fault, say out loud that you are sorry if they feel like you are in their space. Especially give this apology if the activity has been triggered by home renovations. I receive many messages from people whose homes were quiet until they started changing things. Tell the spirits you do not care if they stay, but that they need to get along with the living beings who reside there, too. Many restless spirits respond well to being offered a job. Ask for their help with taking care of the house and in keeping an eye on things. You can butter them up by acknowledging that they know the space better than anyone and that you could really use their help.

This is also a good time to set some ground rules. For example, in my home, I clearly communicate that spirits are not allowed to bother the living while we sleep and that they must stay out of the back of the home where the bedrooms are at night. I use camphor and vapor rub to reinforce the message. Firmly state the ground rules for your space and for the living people who reside there.

Ask the spirits anything you like, such as who they are, how many there are, and, most importantly, what they need. I find that using divination and paranormal investigation tools is very helpful because they can provide external validation for what I perceive with my senses. Tools are not necessary, however. You can simply ask them to speak to you in your mind, by flickering the candle, or even by giving you a sign such as a knock so you know they are there. Take note of the messages you receive and repeat back what you interpreted. You can also ask for knocks or candle flickers to indicate that you interpreted messages correctly. If you get clear messages about what a spirit needs or wants, it is up to you to decide if it is reasonable. Do not make promises you cannot keep. You never know how a spirit will react to an unfulfilled promise, particularly if you are dealing with something like an elemental.

I have a spirit in my home that I have been communicating with and investigating for years. It spends a lot of time in the same room as the mirror I described earlier. For a while, I thought they were the same spirit. I am still not sure if it was ever human or not. Regardless of the type of spirit it may be, they hate it when I play country music while I clean. I figured this out one day when I was doing a deep energetic cleaning. I saw a balloon my son had blown up the day before bounce out of one of our bedrooms. No one else was home except for me and my dogs and we were all in the living room. I brought out my REM Pod and placed it in the room. I muttered something to the effect of, "Things always seem to happen when I listen to country music."

Beeeeeep!

The REM Pod went nuts. I reset it and sat down. I asked if the spirit disliked the country music. *Beeeeep beep beeeeep.*

"Do that again if you like country music." Silence.

"Do you dislike my music? Make that sound if you don't like my music." *BEEEEP!*

Message received.

Dolly Parton and Willie Nelson are two of my favorite musicians. I can't promise I will never play country in the house. After I was done cleaning, I acknowledged out loud that I understood the spirit does not like my taste in music, and I have asked that they share with me what they like to listen to. I am still waiting on an answer. I left a glass of water and a cookie as an apology for playing music they dislike so much. This simple act of kindness bought me an extended period of quiet from a fairly cranky and active spirit.

Once you have said what you need to—and listened for any responses—extinguish the candle and leave the offerings at least overnight. Release your circle and cleanse yourself as described in the six steps. Discard the offerings and water outside the following day, perhaps under a tree or bush, giving them back to nature.

I suggest you observe any differences over the course of one month prior to taking further action.

This Ain't Like the Movies, Folks

Many homes have spirits that are almost unnoticeable to most people because everyone stays in their lane. That is the goal I suggest we aim for when we live in or are regularly spending time in a haunted space. It can be quite difficult to fully dispel an intelligent spirit from what they consider their home. Think of it this way. If a house holds an entity that has resided there for one hundred years or more, or the land beneath the home holds earth spirits that have been there since the beginning of time, or perhaps the house is built upon intersecting ley lines that allow for the opening of multidimensional portals, isn't it a bit arrogant to think that we can shut it all down with ease? Better to start by approaching hauntings with a balance of firmness and empathy than picking a fight you are unlikely to win. While some might consider this discouraging news, I offer it as an exciting opportunity to update one's expectations about what living in a haunted world can be like.

FOLK MAGIC REMEDIES

The following are some more advanced suggestions from different folk magic traditions.

Offering Tasks

Spirits are often viewed as allies in our work in folk magic traditions. If you have a restless spirit in your space that enjoys bothering you as you try to sleep, perhaps they need a task that is well suited to their desire to scare people. As we discussed in chapter 2, a common misconception is that spirits are always bound to one physical location. Ask the spirit in your home if they can leave. If they can, ask for their help in scaring anyone with malicious intent in your neighborhood. If you have spirits that are active around your kids, it could be that they feel protective of children. Task a spirit that wants to be helpful to young people with keeping traffic in order around a school or on the street in front of your home.

Spirit Homes

Another folk magic option is to create a spirit house, which can be a small box, cup, or empty bottle. Imagination and some magical skill come into play here as you envision that whatever vessel you choose is a comfy home for that spirit. You essentially create a mind room for the spirit and anchor it to a physical container. You can add some pretty fabric, dried flowers, or even doll furniture to solidify your creative vision. Tell the spirit that this is a home you prepared just for them and that they are welcome to move into it *if* they don't bother anyone. If the spirit moves in, simply place the vessel in a pleasant but out-of-the-way spot. You can occasionally check in to see if there is anything they need, especially if the spirit begins acting up again. You may find that leaving small offerings of food, water, or fresh flowers periodically keeps them happy.

Spirit Traps

When spirits continue to cause problems in a space, it may be time for a trap. There are all kinds of things that can be used as a spirit trap. Here are a few of my favorites that I learned while studying trolldom:

+ Scorch flax seeds in a pan and spread a line of them outside doors and windows, stating that no spirit may enter unless they cause the seeds to sprout.
+ Create witch bottles that contain broken glass, rusted nails, and other sharp objects. Fill the jars with ammonia or urine and place them outside the window of the afflicted room with the statement that no spirit may enter the space without first navigating the objects in the bottle.
+ Scribble a tangled mess on a paper with the intention that it creates a maze a spirit must solve before entering your space. Hang the paper on the back of a picture facing your front door.

Check your traps periodically and assess whether anything has gotten caught. You can use the psychometry practice from earlier in the chapter to get a sense of whether something has become attached to the trap. If you find something, I find that the best course of action is to leave it there until the spirit's resolve appears to weaken. You can then offer to free them by destroying the trap in exchange for their departure.

Bringing It All Together

Managing spirit activity that you didn't ask for in your home or another space can be challenging and often confusing. It also can make life a lot more interesting and magical. Allow me to share a story that is very close to my heart that will hopefully help bring everything we have covered to life.

Angie's Story

I began my apprenticeship in trolldom in January 2020. When the world shut down due to the COVID-19 pandemic in March 2020, I spent most of my free time practicing folk magic and spirit contact. That is where this particular story begins.

I live in a midcentury ranch that doesn't look like it could ever have spirits, but it is surprisingly active. It appears to have residual energy from one of the original owners, which presented as what sounded like an old man whistling when we first moved in; at least one very old, likely elemental spirit who acts as a caretaker of the home and possibly the surrounding area; and there are spirits who seem to come and go from the space. My mentor taught me a number of different techniques to keep our home clear of disruptive spirits while fostering good relations with the helpful and benevolent ones. However, I struggled to keep a particular spirit out of one of the bedrooms, which led to a lot of fearful nights. There were many times when I would feel someone standing next to the bed as I dozed off or electronics would go off with no provocation. I tried to roll with it, but it eventually became untenable.

In June 2020, I told my mentor I just couldn't get this bedroom free of this one spirit. I told him that every time I began to clear the space, it would present in my mind as a little, laughing, demonlike creature and slip out. We were frequently waking up with bad dreams and things felt very off in our home, so I was eager to address it.

My mentor tuned in to the situation and said he thought we were dealing with the spirit of a teenage girl who was trying to make herself appear scary to get attention. He suggested I make a spirit house for her.

I focused on releasing the fear I had been carrying and began to connect with the presence in the house. I no longer saw a scary demonlike creature. Instead, I found a sour-faced, purple-haired teenage girl. She told me her name was Angie. I decided to make her a spirit house in an old lunch box lined with pretty fabric. I placed it on a shelf in my office, which was in the basement. It appeared that she spent a lot of time sulking down there anyway. I called her in once I was done making her room and offered her some water and a snack. I laid out my ground rules, which were that she was not to disturb the living while we slept, she was not to cause any household problems, and she needed to be nice to our family pets. I then gave her three choices: continue causing problems and be evicted, accept her room and my terms, or let me help her find another family.

She said she "guessed she would stay." I made her agree to each of my terms individually. I then left her in her "room" and exited my office for the night, wondering if I had finally lost my grip on reality.

Over the coming months, I fostered a relationship with the spirit of this surly girl. Angie never gave me enough information to find confirmation of her life or what had caused her death. I picked up enough to know she'd experienced abuse and had run away. She was scared to fully cross over and the prospect of being reconnected with family on the other side was not enticing to her. I do not believe many family members preceded her in death as I perceived that her life ended sometime between the mid-90s to early 2000s. I left her offerings of food and beverages. I visited her every morning and before I went to sleep at night. I left her books and magazines I thought she might find interesting. Once we had a level of trust, I began asking for her help, offering her tasks such as watching out over the neighborhood.

Angie stayed with us until November of that year. There are so many stories from those five months. I would occasionally broach the subject of helping her to fully cross over, but it never went well. She was a hurt teenager who wanted a family, and we were the closest thing she had at that moment. That all changed when a friend of mine booked a virtual tarot reading for her sixteen-year-old daughter, whom I hadn't seen in eight years. Since Angie's spirit house was in my office, I regularly invited her to help with or observe client appointments. I told her that she might find this one interesting because the client was so close to her in age. The reading was delightful and the relationship between mother and daughter was so positive and sweet. The moment the reading was done, I could hear Angie asking if I thought she could have a mom like that if she left and "tried again." I said, "Absolutely!" She told me she was ready to go. I instantly saw an image of a bright light above our heads, and within moments, she was gone.

I would be lying if I said I didn't miss her from time to time, but the thought that a wounded girl would get another chance at a happy family and life where she knows love instead of harm brings me such peace and joy.

I hope this example helped illustrate the way these strategies can work in harmony and that it gets you thinking about creative ways you might handle spirit activity in your own home. I encourage you to journal in your mediumship grimoire on the following prompts:

+ What is your comfort level with sharing a home or another space with a spirit?
+ What are your boundaries of what you will not tolerate?
+ What kinds of tasks can you imagine offering a resident spirit?
+ If you currently live in a haunted location, do you have new ideas of what might improve things?

CHAPTER 10
ETHICAL CONSIDERATIONS

Our final chapter will cover a range of ethical considerations. We will discuss being mindful of our own ethical framework when we are talking with spirits, how to conduct oneself in a graveyard, and tips for finding ethical spiritual professionals and red flags for fraudulent ones.

ESTABLISHING A PERSONAL ETHICAL FRAMEWORK

Sometimes we lose sight of our manners and our ethical grounding when communicating with spirits. Spirits can't clearly stand in front of us, and communication is subject to interpretation. As a result, we can forget we are talking to sovereign beings who deserve to be treated with the same dignity and respect that we would want. In some ways, it is analogous to how easy it is to forget our manners online with people we can't see and are unlikely to encounter in our day-to-day lives.

I find that the two most common ethical missteps in communicating with the spirit world are bullying and provoking spirits into interacting with the living and savior mentality.

Media has set a terrible example of how to interact with spirits, particularly older paranormal investigation shows. When we bully and provoke someone, living or dead, human or inhuman, we can expect to get a negative response. It's not polite and no one wins. Simply be respectful in your communication. Don't provoke, threaten, or shout at the spirits you want to communicate with. They don't owe us anything.

The savior mentality is more complex. A question that frequently arises after making contact with spirits of the dead is how to help them cross over. My response is always whether that is something they asked for. Once again, spirits are independent beings and should be treated as such. Having a savior complex is just as problematic when working with spirits as it is with the living. Most of the time, the desire to help spirits of the dead move on stems from kind and sincere intentions. In our living state, it's hard to fathom why a spirit wouldn't want to leave and, as we've discussed extensively, we don't fully understand why they stay. They likely all need different things and have unique motivations. Some spirits of the dead are clearly ready to move on and will do so with the slightest suggestion, which we'll discuss further on. This is especially true for those who are confused and may not be aware they have died. Others don't want to go and, in my opinion, that's their right if they aren't bothering anyone. Angie, for example, had no interest in leaving until she understood what she could gain if she "tried again." That was her unfinished business. Once it was complete, she moved on with no difficulty.

We must also remember that not all spirits are those of the human dead. We couldn't cross them over in the traditional sense if we tried. In my experience, elemental spirits generally just want to be left alone, higher beings will only get involved when asked, and many conjured spirits can be addressed by consistent cleansing and vibration raising. With the exception of negative entities or conjured spirits who are causing harm to others and will require skilled intervention, the majority of spirits can usually be left to their own devices.

When in Doubt, Ask

You now have the basic skills and steps needed to communicate with the spirit world. When in doubt about the reasons a spirit is still here, it is best to ask directly. Some helpful questions include the following:

- Is there something you need?
- Why are you still here?
- Were you a living person?
- Are you aware you have died?
- Do you like being here?
- Do you want to leave?
- Is there anything you need help with?

These types of questions give spirits of the dead a chance to state what they need on their own terms. Their answers will provide parameters for your role in your interactions with them. If the spirit you are speaking with doesn't indicate that they need help, your place is simply that of the observer. Sometimes the help they request is surprisingly simple. A former student of mine once asked me to speak with spirits in a home she had just moved into. Within moments of arriving, I realized I was sitting in the spot of an older woman who used to live there, and she was not happy about it. She was the primary spirit remaining in the house, and she still liked to sit in "her" spot and look out the windows. She wasn't trapped in the house. She just liked the sunny living room and wanted to have a seat that was reserved for her so she could watch what was going on in the neighborhood. While that wasn't the only thing we learned and addressed that day, that simple message and solution made all the difference. The student wrote to me a week later to say that, after making some adjustments based on what the spirits requested, her house finally felt like home.

It's worth noting that nonhuman spirits like elementals likely won't engage with these types of questions. Negative entities may make up answers and pretend in order to trick you. Always listen to your intuition about whether the answers you receive feel authentic and respond accordingly.

If you do encounter a spirit that is unaware they have died and they want to move on, it is likely that the exit is right in front of them. They might only need a gentle suggestion in order to see it, much like the encounter with the elderly woman who died of Alzheimer's I described earlier. Here are some basic steps you can take to help a willing spirit cross over.

+ Ask the spirit if there is someone who preceded them in death whom they wish they could see again.
+ If the answer is yes, ask them if they see a door or a light above them.
+ Tell them their loved one is waiting beyond the light or door.

You will be surprised how many willing spirits move on with this simple suggestion. However, if they choose to not move forward, don't push it. Set boundaries and call in a professional if you feel like that is needed.

Reflecting on Your Own Ethics

Please journal in your mediumship grimoire on the following.

+ Are there times you have pushed spirits to interact with you? How do you feel about that now?
+ Are there times you wanted to rescue or help a spirit you encountered?
+ What does it feel like when offers to help are rejected or left unanswered?

You may also find it helpful to write down your own personal code of ethics as a medium. You might include statements such as, "I will treat all spirits as sovereign beings," or, "I will treat all spirits I encounter with kindness." This process can help you crystallize values you can fall back on when you encounter tricky situations. For example, I was once asked on a podcast that was hosted by two famous musicians. They wanted to find a medium who would conduct a séance so they could contact dead celebrities. The hosts were very nice, and I would have reached a wide audience by doing the show, but I didn't feel comfortable cold-calling spirits of the dead for entertainment. I decided to turn down the opportunity because this fell outside my personal code of ethics, which includes that I use my mediumship skills to help people build respectful relationships with spirits of the dead.

GRAVEYARD ETIQUETTE

If you communicate with spirits of the dead, it is likely you will eventually spend some time in cemeteries and graveyards. They are peaceful and usually filled with mature trees and plants. The headstones and mausoleums are often intricate and beautiful and tell a visual story of the area's residents and history. It's also just spooky enough to be fun. The dead can also be quite chatty in their final resting place, which makes it a great place to practice. Every graveyard is different, as they are all influenced by the spirits that inhabit them and the lives they lived. Spending time in graveyards can be downright magical. However, it is important to know that these powerful spaces are another world from our own. When the living choose to enter, we need to behave ourselves and be willing to play by different rules ... or potentially experience some consequences.

Graveyards are burial sites that are connected to a church, while cemeteries are not. However, the terms are often used interchangeably. For our purposes, we will use the term *graveyard*. In my opinion, it is best to approach all burial sites as consecrated, hallowed ground. The following tips come from years of trial and error in my personal practice. I am grateful to have had the benefit of learning from other experienced spiritual workers, particularly those who work in the conjure and hoodoo traditions of the Southern United States.[27]

For context, let me tell you about how I used to mosey around graveyards. I would waltz straight in, usually with my coffee and occasionally on the phone with a friend. I would read aloud from the headstones as I wandered, occasionally stopping to lean against one and take a selfie. You may be wondering, what's the big deal? Quite a bit, as it turns out, and I am glad I know better now. I'll explain as we go through this brief overview of how to conduct yourself responsibly and respectfully in the resting place of the dead.

The Graveyard Gates

It all starts at the entrance. All graveyards, whether they are formally consecrated or not, are designated as a final resting place of the deceased. Those gates have guardians. It is best to pay your respect on your way in. Plan to pour some water, coffee, or alcohol at the entrance and ask for permission to enter. You can also leave some unwrapped candy and coins as payment. Think of it this way. If you call on someone at home, it is polite to bring a gift such as flowers, food, or a bottle of wine. We don't just walk into people's homes uninvited, unannounced, and empty-handed just because the door is open. You do not need to leave offerings upon exiting, but it's always polite to say, "Thank you."

---

27. I offer many thanks to the elders and teachers of the Mile High Conjure Gala over the years as well as the Gala's founder, Loretta Ledesma. Many of my foundational lessons came from these events.

Cover Your Head

Wear a hat or headscarf in the graveyard. The tops of our heads are energetic portals. They are like a beacon of light for the dead. Covering our heads provides a layer of protection for this powerful and vulnerable place on our body.

Don't Read the Headstones Aloud

When you point to and say the name of a dead human, their spirit wakes up. If you don't acknowledge that you called them and dismiss them politely and accordingly, they will follow you around wondering why you disturbed them. I used to love to wander through rows of headstones, pointing and reading the names and dates of death of the people buried there. I would also find that the longer I walked, the heavier I began to feel. Once when walking through the cemetery in my hometown, I felt a pulling on one side of my body. I literally felt like someone was hanging on to my shoulder. I believe that I woke up one or more spirits who were pulling on my arm, trying to get me to acknowledge them. It breaks my heart to consider how it might feel to be ignored by the first person to speak your name in years. Out of respect, it is best to only utter the names of spirits you want to talk to while in the graveyard.

Remember These Are Resting Places

Burial plots are the beds of the dead. I'm likely not the only one who's walked up to a headstone to take a selfie, my feet directly over the head of the body buried beneath. I doubt many of us enjoy being jostled and stomped on when we are sleeping. Sometimes, particularly in old or especially crowded graveyards, it is difficult to avoid walking over where bodies lie. Do your best and give your pardons as needed.

Build Relationships with the Dead

As you continue to grow your spirit communication practice, consider making a friend or two in your local graveyard. You can research notable people who are buried there who have a connection to your life or interests. As you build your relationship, ask for details about their lives and try to verify them later. This is a great way to test your skills. As the spirit begins to know and trust you, you can also ask for assistance if needed. As we have discussed, the dead often appreciate being offered tasks. This is a common practice in folk magic traditions as the mighty dead can be tremendous allies in our work. Don't jump right to the quizzing and asking for favors, though. Build the relationship by bringing small offerings such as water, alcohol, coffee, flowers, money, tobacco, or snacks. As you begin to know the spirit, your offerings can get more specific to their tastes and personalities. More importantly, simply spend time talking and listening. Always remember to set your boundaries as you would in any relationship. At a minimum, make sure they understand you don't wish to be followed home or visited unannounced.

No Touching, No Taking

Graveyards are powerful places for magical work. The more time you spend in graveyards, the more you will notice. There will be the expected flowers and mementos from recent funerals and family visits. However, you may look up and notice trinkets and unusual things hanging in or nailed to the trunks of trees. You will notice things placed on headstones, such as arrangements of cigarettes, jewelry, money, liquor, and papers bound in twine. These are signs of magical workings. Don't touch or take anything you may come across, no matter how tempting it may be. We pay for anything we take or disturb in the graveyard, one way or another.

Use Your Spirit Communication Steps

Last but not least, use visits to the graveyard as an opportunity to practice. You have the tools to talk to spirits. Put these skills to use in all possible settings, especially when visiting somewhere as powerful and mysterious as the graveyard. Practice steps 1 through 3 prior to entering. When you are ready to leave, state that no one is allowed to follow you home. Practice step 6 after exiting the graveyard and prior to getting into your car or entering your home.

FINDING ETHICAL SPIRITUAL WORKERS

You are more than capable of handling 99 percent of the spirit encounters you will have. We all get in over our heads sometimes, however. If you find yourself facing spirit activity that makes you feel unsafe or is escalating or if you simply want another opinion, it's time to find an ethical, experienced spiritual worker. Before we discuss how to find the good ones, I want to address some things to watch out for.

The potential for fraud in mediumship and spirit communication is high. People seeking these services are often experiencing grief and are therefore more vulnerable. Unfortunately, there are a lot of people who have been scammed by so-called spiritual professionals. This damages all of us. I was once on my way to a tattoo appointment and stopped for a cup of coffee nearby. I got to chatting with the barista, who turned out to be the owner. It somehow came up that I was a tarot reader, and he told me he hadn't had a great experience with getting his cards read. Several years ago, he was freshly out of a rocky relationship and stopped at a walk-in shop. The kind that has a neon Psychic ~ Fortunes Read Here ~ Tarot sign ... the type of which I fully admit to coveting. He got a reading that felt fairly accurate for 60 dollars, which is a standard beginner rate for most readers. At the end of his reading, however, the woman told him that his ex had laid a curse on him. She said she was happy to remove it—for an additional 500 dollars. He paid it and she supposedly removed the curse. In doing so, she claimed she discovered another issue that would cost even more. Thankfully, this very nice small business owner did not work with this woman again. He had been conned, and the experience had left him justifiably suspicious of all other psychics, mediums, and readers. I offered him my sincere apologies on behalf of all decent spiritual workers and tried not to show how angry and horrified I was by his story. Unfortunately, it was not the first time nor the worst example I'd heard of blatant fraud.

Serious and dedicated practitioners are significantly impacted by the stereotypes these scammers perpetuate. We spend years studying and honing our skills in addition to paying taxes, running our websites, marketing our services, jumping through all the hoops of small business ownership, and enduring the smirks and cynicism of those who think we are full of it. For us, these frauds and con artists are downright offensive. Here are some tips on how to spot the scammers.

General Red Flags

Unclear pricing. A spiritual worker who is not forthcoming about their prices should be approached with suspicion. That suspicion should be compounded if the person keeps finding issues that only they can fix at an ever-increasing price.

Unable or unwilling to describe their background. We're living in an interesting time when there are schools and certification programs for spiritual and occult arts. Many people are still self-taught, learning from a combination of websites, dusty books in metaphysical shops, one-off classes, and lots and lots of practice. I believe one is not inherently better than the other. However, when we take the step of charging for our services, we need to be forthcoming about our backgrounds, education, and experience. If you seek services from someone who dodges your questions or takes offense because you want more information, you may want to rethink their trustworthiness. Similarly, if a spiritual worker claims to receive all their information and knowledge "directly from spirit," which is also frequently referred to as downloads, that is another clue the person may be fraudulent. While serious practitioners do frequently receive information from the spiritual realm, we also need to study folklore, history, and the technical specifics of our trade.

Claim they can cure major health issues like cancer and HIV. Magic can create incredible change in people's lives, but anyone who claims they can cure serious or terminal illnesses should always be approached with caution.

BRIGHT RED SOCIAL MEDIA FLAGS

There are a few hallmark red flags to watch out for in social media spaces such as Instagram, Facebook, and TikTok. Almost every medium, tarot reader, psychic, and astrologer I know uses social media to promote their business and connect with current and potential clients and students. Social media has been a fantastic catalyst for many spiritual workers. Unfortunately, fraud is currently rampant. If you pay attention, you can avoid the scammers with ease. Here's what to look out for:

They solicit you. Many of us who are open to spiritual topics and spend time on social media have had the experience of opening our DMs to discover a message that starts with something like, "Grand rising, beautiful! I was drawn to your profile because of your energy, and I would like to offer you a reading." No ethical reader will solicit you for a reading. We allow potential clients to contact us.

They want payment through an app and their handle doesn't match their social media information. Reputable workers generally direct clients to their websites to set up appointments. Even those who do not have websites will provide clear instructions of how to send payment and confirm appointments. If a supposed spiritual worker slides into your DMs and asks for payment directly to Venmo or Cash App, but their payment information doesn't match their social media profile, that's a red flag.

You are followed by an account you recognize ... but something seems off. Unfortunately, most upstanding readers have been victims of identity theft on social media. Scammers will steal the pictures and text from a social media account to create a lookalike or copycat account. This is particularly a problem on Instagram. You will notice the pictures have all been posted within a few days of each other and often lack captions. The number of account followers will be either much lower than what you remember or much higher. This is often due to services that allow people to purchase followers. The primary clue to spotting a copycat account, however, is in the spelling of the account name. It will always be slightly off with an extra letter or period or a different spelling. It's rarely helpful to notify the person whose identity has been stolen as there is little they can do. The first thing the fraudulent account typically does is block the person they are impersonating. The best thing you can do is to report the account and block them immediately.

Unfortunately, social media companies have been slow to address this issue, so it is on us to be smart consumers. Remember to trust your intuition. If something doesn't feel right, it probably isn't.

FINDING AN ETHICAL SPIRITUAL WORKER

There have been several times throughout this book when I have referred to situations that may call for an ethical, professional spiritual worker. Things like living in a haunted house or suspecting you have a spirit attachment can feel overwhelming, and it's ok to ask for help from someone who understands. There will also be times when you fumble in doing this work, whether it is accidently offending an elemental spirit that is now making mischief in your life or not closing a séance fully and finding you have a wayward spirit living in your basement. The mistakes we can make while doing this work are infinite because we can't totally understand what we are dealing with. Don't let embarrassment or fear stand in the way of getting the help you need. That applies not just to spiritual matters, but just about every other aspect of our lives. Now that you know some things to look out for, let's talk about how to find ethical and trustworthy practitioners.

Be Clear on What You Need

Do your best to get specific about what you need. Our global and connected world is both a blessing and a curse. You have almost infinite options, but that doesn't mean all of them are a fit for your unique circumstances. The clearer you can become on what it is you want and need, the easier it will be to vet the options available to you.

Visit Your Local Metaphysical Shops or Botanicas

It's always helpful to have a medium, tarot reader, astrologer, or psychic you can see in-person. It's also important to support our local magical communities. If you do not have a space like this or the options available to you don't have what you are looking for, social media is a great resource. There are many wonderful shops that have an online presence. Many of them have house readers or spiritual workers who see clients virtually and even teach classes.

Ask Around

It's always a good idea to vet anyone you are considering working with. Ask other people if they have worked with them and what their experience was like. If you are considering a worker whom you have no connections with, do some internet searches to see if you can find reviews or testimonials that can speak to the quality of their work.

Listen to Your Instincts

Trust and comfortability are crucial when you hire someone to help you with spiritual matters. For example, if you want to hire someone to help address a troublesome spirit in your home, it is important you feel emotionally and physically safe with that person. The best spiritual workers help their clients feel empowered by providing strategies and tools to address difficult issues. On the other hand, there are unscrupulous spiritual professionals who keep their clients coming back by convincing them they are helpless. Go with a worker who helps you tap into your power, not one who is only interested in their own.

It's Okay to Say No if You Feel Uncomfortable

Please remember you always have the right to say no to anything you are uncomfortable with when receiving spiritual services. Here's an example from the practitioner's side. I once had a client who needed help with a spirit that was scaring the people who lived in the home. We set up an appointment, and I was prepared to hold séance space so we could connect with the spirit and identify how everyone could move forward. When the appointment started, it was clear the client was very nervous about this plan, even though we had agreed to it ahead of time. It turned out that what the client really needed was an opportunity to tell someone who believed them about their experiences. Because I do this work all the time, I was eager to get to the heart of the issue. However, it would have been wrong of me to push the client into something they weren't ready for. You always have the right to state your boundaries and to change the plan if you are not comfortable.

IN CLOSING

If you ever find yourself with ethical questions in your mediumship practice, start by coming back to the classic golden rule of treating others as you would want to be treated. Conversely, you should also expect to be treated as well as you are willing to treat others. You can be kind and respectful and also maintain your boundaries, a philosophy that applies to living and nonliving beings alike.

CONCLUSION

You now have the knowledge and skills to talk to spirits. I hope you've had some truly weird and wonderful experiences by this point. I encourage you to sit down with your mediumship grimoire and reflect on how far you have come! Feel proud of yourself. Not everyone is as brave or inquisitive as you have proven to be.

Personally, I have found that connection with the spirit realm and knowing there is more to come after we leave our bodies help me be brave, take chances, and to not sweat the small stuff. I hope learning to talk to spirits will continue to spark your curiosity, make your life more magical, and leave you forever changed.

BIBLIOGRAPHY

Bood, Deena. "Tommyknockers." Bella Online: The Voice of Women. Accessed December 23, 2021. http://www.bellaonline.com/articles/art58728.asp.

Campbell, Joseph. *Hero with a Thousand Faces*. New York: Pantheon Books, 1968.

"The Changing Global Religious Landscape." Pew Research Center. April 5, 2017. https://www.pewforum.org/2017/04/05/the-changing-global-religious-landscape/.

"Colorado Gold Rush." *Colorado Encyclopedia*. Accessed December 22, 2021. https://coloradoencyclopedia.org/article/colorado-gold-rush.

The Editors of *Encyclopedia Britannica*. "Phoenix." *Encyclopedia Britannica*. November 17, 2021. https://www.britannica.com/topic/phoenix-mythological-bird.

———. "Siren." *Encyclopedia Britannica*. May 7, 2020. https://www.britannica.com/topic/Siren-Greek-mythology.

Lebling, Robert. *Legends of the Fire Spirits: Jinn and Genies from Arabia to Zanzibar*. London: I. B. Tauris, 2015.

Lucas, Teghan, and Maciej Henneberg. "Are Human Faces Unique? A Metric Approach to Finding Single Individuals without Duplicates in Large Samples." *Forensic Science International* (2015): 257 .10.1016/j.forsciint.2015.09.003.

Mills, Billy. "The Old Straight Track by Alfred Watkins—Walking Through the Past." *The Guardian*. Accessed April 16, 2022. https://www.theguardian.com/books/booksblog/2015/aug/20/the-old-straight-track-by-alfred-watkins-walking-through-the-past.

Newton, Michael. *Journey of Souls: Case Studies of Life Between Lives*. Woodbury, MN: Llewellyn Publications, 2002.

Owen, Iris M., and Margaret Sparrow. *Conjuring Philip: An Adventure in Psychokinesis*. New York: Pocket Book, 1977.

Perron, Andrea. *House of Darkness, House of Light: The True Story*. Bloomington, IN: Author House, 2011.

Petruzzello, M. "Roman Catholic Saints." *Encyclopedia Britannica*. Accessed November 29, 2021. https://www.britannica.com/story/roman-catholic-saints-hallowed-from-the-other-side/.

Pinkola Estés, Clarissa. *Untie the Strong Woman: Blessed Mother's Immaculate Love for the Wild Soul*. Louisville, CO: Sounds True Publishing, 2011.

Redish, Lauren, and Orrin Lewis. "Gluscabi and the Wind Eagle (Abenaki Northeast Woodlands)." Native Languages of the Americas. Accessed January 30, 2022. https://www.angelfire.com/ia2/stories3/wind.html.

Temkin, C. L. *Four Treatises of Theophrastus von Hohenheim, Called Paracelsus*. United Kingdom: Johns Hopkins University Press, 1996.

Weisberg, Barbara. *Talking to the Dead: Kate and Maggie Fox and the Rise of Spiritualism*. San Francisco, CA: HarperOne, 2005.

RECOMMENDED READING LIST

Belanger, Michelle. *The Dictionary of Demons: Tenth Anniversary Edition: Names of the Damned*. Woodbury, MN: Llewellyn Publications, 2020.

Buckland, Raymond. *Book of Spirit Communications*. Woodbury, MN: Llewellyn Publications, 2004.

Echols, Damien. *Angels and Archangels: A Magician's Guide*. Louisville, CO: Sounds True Publishing, 2020.

Gårdbäck, Johannes Björn. *Trolldom: Spells and Methods of the Norse Folk Magic Tradition*. Forestville, CA: Yronwode Institution, 2015.

Mikaharic, Draja. *Materia Magica*. Morrisville, NC: Lulu, 2010.

———. *Spiritual Cleansing: A Handbook of Psychic Self-Protection*. Newburyport, MA: Weiser Books, 2003.

Moise, Hoodoo Sen. *Working Conjure: A Guide to Hoodoo Folk Magic*. Newburyport, MA: Weiser Books, 2018.